IN THE FOO
OF
ALEXANDER CORDELL

IN THE FOOTSTEPS
OF
ALEXANDER CORDELL

Chris Barber

BLORENGE BOOKS

First published 2007

ISBN 1 872730 12 4
ISBN 9 781872730 12 7

BLORENGE BOOKS

Blorenge Cottage, Church Lane, Llanfoist,
Abergavenny, Gwent NP7 9NG
Tel: 01873 856114

Website: www.blorenge-books.co.uk

Printed by MWL Print Group Ltd, Units 12/13,
Pontyfelin Industrial Estate, Pontypool, Gwent NP4 0DG.
Tel: 01495 750033

"I stood before the rusted grates of tumble-down cottages; touched scraps of faded wallpaper and tried to recapture the laughter and tears of a village that had died; the clang of the pots on ovens, the scrape of hobnails, quarrellings and whispered love. I realised that here on this hillside was the story of a people who were now but dust, but by courage and labour had built an industry, which had now also vanished. The village was called Garnddyrys and it was once a thriving community, a little town of people who lived their lives on the edge of a golden valley."

Alexander Cordell

ACKNOWLEDGEMENTS

I am most grateful to everyone who has assisted with the production of this book which has been compiled over a period of more than twenty years. Special thanks are due to Michael Blackmore for his artwork Ann Waller and Anne Marie Lawrence are both thanked for proof reading the finished manuscript and making suggestions for improvements.

This book is dedicated to Anne Marie with grateful thanks for her encouragement, support and for becoming a very important part of my life, since our first meeting on the Blorenge Mountain.

CONTENTS

Alexander Cordell at Sirhowy Ironworks in 1985

INTRODUCTION

In 1979 I came to live in the village of Llanfoist below the brooding mass of the Blorenge mountain and after spending a few months carrying out improvements to my cottage I began to explore the local countryside. In particular I tramped the numerous paths and tracks that ascend and criss-cross the Blorenge and gradually got to know the area intimately. But as I walked, I began to hear voices - no, I wasn't going mad, or going through some kind of religious experience - but imagining the larger than life characters in Alexander Cordell's *Rape of the Fair Country* - walking the same routes that I was following. As I crossed the bracken clad slopes I found myself listening to the rumble of horse-drawn trams loaded with limestone or pig iron and when I stood on the site of Garnddyrys Forge I tried to imagine the whine of the rolling mill.

By the Balance Pond, below Pwll-du, I pictured young Iestyn Mortymer having a scrap with Mosen Jenkins beneath a swinging lantern suspended from a pole. Then descending to Llanfoist Wharf, I conjured up a picture of the Garnddyrys villagers riding the trams down the steep inclines to pile into the waiting narrow boats for their annual outing to Newport Fair.

An idea was taking shape in my mind and having previously written some walking guides to the Brecon Beacons National Park, I decided that I would now like to write a book describing walks on the Blorenge and the surrounding area. It would be appropriate to link it with Cordell's *Rape of the Fair Country*, thus providing a historical and literary background to some of the locations featured in this popular novel. Published in 1959 it was an immediate success and translated into seventeen languages it sold over a million copies. During his life-time Alexander Cordell wrote thirty books, but he will always mainly be remembered for *Rape of the Fair Country*.

Set in the turbulent times of the Industrial Revolution, in 19th century Monmouthshire, it tells the story, through the eyes of Iestyn Mortymer, of the ironmaking communities of Blaenafon, Garnddyrys and Nantyglo. The exciting tale culminates in the Chartists' uprising and their historic march on Newport in November 1839.

I wrote an enthusiastic letter to Alexander Cordell, who was living on the Isle of Man at that time, and put my idea to him, seeking his approval and permission to include some quotations from his work. I tentatively suggested that I might call my book *Cordell Country* and would be most grateful if he could write a foreword. He wrote back, return of post. and said "Yes, I like both the idea and the title. I will certainly write you a foreword and give you any help that I can."

For the next three years I researched my project, walked and re-walked the various circular routes that I had devised; occasionally talking to elderly people who had been born in the area, seeking their memories and anecdotes. I also acquired copies of old photographs depicting industrial scenes and took many present day pictures of various relics and the beautiful scenery in this area.

Gradually the book took shape and I then paid a visit to Michael Blackmore, a well known Abergavenny artist, who kindly agreed to undertake a set of drawings illustrating scenes from the novel and some historical re-constructions. This was the beginning of a much valued friendship and since that time we have worked together on numerous projects.

One evening in 1984 I read in the *South Wales Argus* that Alexander Cordell had been invited to visit Chepstow to unveil a plaque marking the spot, beside the River Wye, where the three Chartist leaders, John Frost, William Jones and Zephaniah Williams (sentenced to transportation in 1839), had boarded a steam boat called *Usk* to begin their long journey to Van Dieman's Land - Tasmania.

I mingled with the crowd and took pictures of Cordell performing the unveiling ceremony. When he had finished his brief speech, I went over

and introduced myself. Alex expressed his pleasure at meeting me and we then walked to a nearby cafe for a pot of tea. During our conversation, I showed him my draft manuscript and some of the illustrations. His reaction was very favourable and he told me that he was delighted that I was working on this project.

Alexander Cordell unveiling a plaque marking the spot, beside the River Wye, where in 1839 the three Chartist leaders, John Frost, William Jones and Zephaniah Williams boarded a steam boat called *Usk* to begin their long journey to Van Dieman's Land - Tasmania.

In due course Alex sent me his foreword to the book, which read as follows:

"In 1954 I unloaded on to an unsuspecting public my first novel, one which was supposed to set the Thames on fire. In fact it earned just one-and-sixpence less than the royalty advance of £75 paid to me by the unfortunate publisher.

My form of transport in those days was a pedal-assisted auto-cycle which took me daily from Llanelen village to my work as a Civil Servant. I set about trying to be a better Civil Servant, but failed because the writer's bug began to bite me again. And one winter's night saw me standing near the *Old Victoria Inn* wondering what bomb had hit this area. It was clear that something had violated this once fair country.

A man came walking with a bicycle out of the cold moonlight and he said his name was Parry; that he was a local postman on his way to visit his sister. I asked him what had happened to the place he called Garnddyrys.

'Jawch, mun - terrible things have happened up here, don't you know?' I said I didn't, and Mr. Parry suggested that I should meet him the next evening at *The Rolling Mill*, a pub in Blaenafon. Next evening I was there at the appointed time, but Mr. Parry did not come. Some colliers, wondering at the stranger in their midst, engaged me in conversation: it isn't that the Welsh are nosey, they only want to know what's happening. I told them I was waiting for Mr. Parry, the postman.

'Duw', exclaimed a collier, 'haven't you heard, mun? He died last night on his way to see his sister'.

And so began scores of interviews with the old people whose tales of Blaenafon's past breathed life into *Rape of the Fair Country*. I wrote the book at white heat, scarcely altering a chapter: in between spells of writing I studied at the University of Wales, Aberystwyth, and befriended every available librarian; more, I suddenly discovered that hand in hand with the tale of the mountain town went the last bloody revolution in Britain, the Chartist Rebellion, when men like John Frost a hundred years before their time, fought and suffered for the Six Point Charter - five of which we enjoy today in freedom."

Cordell Country was launched two months later at the Angel Hotel in Abergavenny with about one hundred guests present, including Alexander Cordell and his wife who had flown over from the Isle of Man for the occasion. In order to entertain my guests, I had put together an audio-visual presentation relating to the area that I had named *Cordell Country*.

I remember Alex was sitting in the front row and as my slide presentation finished, I looked across at him and saw tears rolling down his cheeks. He was obviously very moved by the occasion, for here was I paying tribute to a literary masterpiece that he had created nearly thirty years previously. Before getting to his feet to speak to the audience, he had to quickly compose himself. Everyone was waiting with much anticipation and the atmosphere in the room was quite electric.

Alex began by expressing his pleasure in returning to Abergavenny for this very special evening and how thrilled he was that this corner of Wales was to become known as 'Cordell Country'. The tribute was much appreciated for it marked a very important period in his life.

Terry Campbell, a *Western Mail* journalist was present in the audience and a few days later his paper contained a three-quarter page review of *Cordell Country*. He commented:

> "Those hills will never be the same again. A writer has shared his vision with us. The mountains now ring out the message of their bruised and battered, tearful and joyful past which comes echoing down the years from that cruel anvil, the industrial revolution of the 19th century.
>
> *Cordell Country* in discovering the heritage of the ironmaking communities immortalised in *Rape of the Fair Country* enlightens and educates at the same time, as it points you on your way."

Within six months *Cordell Country* went into a second edition and a total of eight thousand copies were sold. My endeavours had resulted in large numbers of people returning time and time again to explore this fascinating area. Educational groups in particular have found the book most useful and many schools have used it as the basis for environmental projects relating to the Industrial Revolution.

Numerous letters of appreciation were also received from local people and also visitors who travelled to Gwent from distant parts. Many came to study the industrial history of the area, whilst others who had read and re-read *Rape of the Fair Country* came to seek and enjoy the geography of the story.

Comments on *Cordell Country*

"*Cordell Country* in discovering the heritage of the ironmaking communities immortalised in *Rape of the Fair Country* enlightens and educates at the same time, as it points you on your way."

Terry Campbell *Western Mail* 1985

"Inspired by Cordell's seductive prose and Chris Barber's own obvious spiritual affinity with the countryside he describes, the reader at home or out tracing the recommended paths is utterly captivated. The illustrations by Michael Blackmore are great."

Mike Rice, *South Wales Argus* 1985

The *Cordell Country Inn* with its original sign, which was unfortunately stolen

Reconstruction of Blaenafon Ironworks by Michael Blackmore

I had published *Cordell Country* in 1985 and as the years slipped by, some of the content of the book gradually became out of date for a number of changes occurred in the area. In 1986 a long closed public house (the *Royal Oak*), situated high on the side of the Blorenge, was re-opened and re-named the *Cordell Country Inn*. This name was inspired by the title of my book and for a brief time it displayed two sign boards, painted by Michael Blackmore, which reproduced the book cover. Unfortunately within a short time one sign was stolen and the other vandalised, so these are no longer in place.

Restoration work at Blaenavon Ironworks made steady progress and guided tours of the site became available. Big Pit Colliery which had closed in 1980 was turned into a visitor attraction and is now the National Mining Museum of Wales. A steam railway run by volunteers was opened to provide rides from Furnace Sidings, near Big Pit, to the *Whistle Inn* at Garn-yr-erw, where a new station was built.

At Nantyglo, the site of Crawshay Bailey's mansion known as Ty Mawr, was excavated and the adjoining Round Towers renovated.

The Workmen's Hall & Institute in Park Street, Blaenafon, was restored in 1990 and in 2001 the old Council Offices in Lion Street were given a new lease of life to provide a very fine new library and a heritage centre containing an exhibition on the life of Alexander Cordell.

In November 2000 Blaenafon and its surrounding landscape was designated a World Heritage Site. My guidebook entitled *Exploring Blaenavon Industrial Landscape World Heritage Site* was published in June 2002.

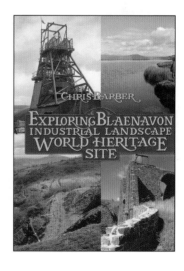

Alexander Cordell working on one of his many books

Keeper's Pond is a beautiful location in 'Cordell Country'

"I thought of my river, the Afon-lwyd, that my father had fished in youth, with rod and line for the leaping salmon under the drooping alders. The alders, he said, that fringed the banks ten deep, planted by the wind of the mountains. But no salmon in the river now, for it is black with furnace washings and slag, and the great silver fish have been beaten back to the sea or gasped out their lives on sands of coal. No alders stand now for they have been chopped as fuel for the cold blast. Even the mountains are shells, groaning in their hollows of emptiness, trembling to the arrows of the pit-props in their sides, bellowing down the old workings that collapse in unseen dust five hundred feet below.

Plundered is my country, violated, raped."

RAPE OF THE FAIR COUNTRY

Alexander Cordell will always be associated with Blaenafon and the surrounding area, for his novel *Rape of the Fair Country* became an international best seller when it was first published in 1959.

Set in the turbulent times of the Industrial Revolution in 19th century Monmouthshire, the book tells the story of the fictitious Mortymer family and the ironmaking communities of Blaenafon, Garnddyrys and Nantyglo.

Alexander Cordell always undertook meticulous research before writing his many novels, and many people would agree that no other writer has managed to capture the atmosphere and spirit of 19th century industrial Wales so well.

In January 1959, Cordell commented that he was "astonished" at the success of the book:

> " I have been completely upended. One moment I was in obscurity, the next projected into the glaring limelight. I did not think that the book would go down that well. I expected it to cover costs but nothing more. I wrote it sincerely and with everything in me for I love Wales and its people.
>
> All my life I have dabbled with writing, even as a child. But it was after the war, when I needed a means of expression, that I began to write seriously. My first attempt was successful - a short story called *The Diver's Wife*, which sold for two and a half guineas in 1949. My wife and I were so thrilled, that on the proceeds we took a couple of friends out to dinner. Since then I have sold literally hundreds of short stories to all types of magazines.
>
> It was Rose who made me write one-act plays for the Llanelen branch of the Womens' Institute They have already performed *The Witnesses*, and *Tea at Pye Corner*, another link with the Chartists is being rehearsed for this year's W.I. drama festival.
>
> I was never happy anywhere till I came to Wales and I am really sorry that I am not Welsh. In the Welsh people I have found a frankness, friendliness, hospitality and industry that I have found nowhere else."

What the critics said about *Rape of the Fair Country*

"In this book there is a vitality that I have found in very few books during my time. This shocking book is anything but sad. The writing anything but crude. There are patches of poetic prose which are a joy and there is an abundance of rich humour."

Jack Jones

"The book is a real shaker and the untidy anguish that nourishes the dreams of our nameless ones can rarely have received so vivid a tribute."

Gwyn Thomas

"It is a tremendous book, an exciting book - I shall be astonished if this novel is not universally regarded as one of the outstandng literary events of the year."

Aneurin Bevan

"I am most grateful that the whole British Press seems to have confirmed my initial judgement on the book. Books such as this only come once in a lifetime.

What can you say about a good book except that it is good and deserves to be widely read - as I have no doubt it will be. I have returned to the book since my first reading for the sheer joy of the comic scenes and the picturesque descriptive writing."

Jack Jones

"His chapters are bursting with vitality, zest, gusto. His fighting and love-making - and there is plenty of both - are on a Homeric scale. It is wonderfully alive. And the whole wide scene of the ravaged countryside, with the moor and mountain looking down on the furnaces, pitheads and hovels, is all solidly and beautifully there. To all readers except those who have been running away from life so long they cannot stop, I recommend, most warmly and gratefully, *Rape of the Fair Country*."

J. B. Priestley

Weary after a hectic ten days of interviews, recordings, posing for photographs and autograph signings, Cordell was aware of some of the criticisms that the book had received. He commented, "I agree that in many places the book is tough and not for the squeamish. It is the writer's business to tell the truth as he sees it - the truth of people who laboured in darkness."

Rape of the Fair Country shot to the top of the best-seller list in Britain and was there for several weeks. It went into Book Clubs from Britain to South Africa and there were a score of translations on both sides of the Iron Curtain.

> "It is the book-of-the month in South Africa and a similar designation is being considered for it in the United States. This book which deals with the life of a family and a community in North Monmouthshire in the 1830s cries out for filming."
>
> Western Mail January 1959

On January 16th 1959, The *Western Mail* announced that it had bought the serial rights of *Rape of the Fair Country*, which critics were universally hailing as "something more than a best-seller."

In April 1959 the book was published in America under the clumsy title *The Rape of the Fair Country.*

"One of the finest novels of its kind since *How Green Was My Valley* ... and I think, far superior to it. A novel of astonishing gusto and, despite the savagery of its theme, one that is distinguished by the richness of its humour. This, believe me is a book!

Victor P. Haas, Chicago *Tribune*

"There is a passion in the writing and the living which communicates itself to the reader as do the shifting moods and glorious imagery, the steadfastness of men and even the fears they can engender. This is an exceptional novel of depth as well as height, of beauty, realism, and heart."

Alice Dixton Bond, Boston *Herald*

The Rape of the Fair Country is centered in the Mortymer family, whose head, respected by the townfolk, was in his way a philosopher and guide. The narrator, his son, tells the story of the increasing strife, the fear and the hatred when fatal attempts were made to organize the Welsh laborers into hopeless unions. In the midst of despair, brutality and tragedy Mr Cordell has created an atmosphere of tenderness and gaiety, with moments of ecstasy. He has the extraordinary ability to fascinate and startle the reader into laughter."

Harrison Smith for the *Saturday Review*

"How to describe Mr Cordell's strange, beautiful, and moving book? How to suggest the powerful spell it lays upon one's imagination? Perhaps it would be best to say that he has filled his pages with a wild Welsh poetry as authentic as anything Dylan Thomas ever wrote; that he has told as exciting and tragically violent a tale as ever recorded... yet somehow made his novel a hymn to the glory of life itself."

Orville Prescott, New York *Times*

Back in 1940, Richard Llewellyn published a novel called *How Green was My Valley*. Until the appearance of *The Rape of the Fair Country*, the Llewellyn novel was without a real rival in the field of fiction about Welsh miners. Now it has not only been rivalled but surpassed, for Mr Cordell's is a novel of unique power and readability.

This is a novel of man's inhumanity to man and yet, if you will believe me, this is also one of the most richly humorous novels we have had in many a day. It bubbles with the juices of life and is told with enormous gusto."

Omaha *World Herald*

The Film that was never made

In 1960 Alexander Cordell sold the film rights to *Rape of the Fair Country* for £30,000 which he put into trust for his daughter, who subsequently married and went to live in Finland. Among the seventeen film offers made to the author were ones by Stanley Baker and Lew Grade. The well known actors Richard Burton, Siân Phillips, Hugh Griffiths and, despite her lack of acting experience, singer Mary Hopkin were all suggested as likely stars. The idea was even put forward that Tom Jones could appear in it. He would certainly have been suitable for he, at that time, was the absolute epitome of what Iestyn Mortymer might have looked like.

Cordell commented: "I spent nearly three years writing the book, but completed the film script in just over a fortnight. I was delighted with the idea of Stanley Baker playing the part of Hywel Mortymer for he would have just walked into the role like a giant."

In October 1967 a film company based in London paid a visit to Blaenafon to assess possible locations in the area where the novel was set. They liked what they saw and even drew up plans to 'reconstruct' the blast furnaces at the old ironworks. Fortunately the adjoining cottages known as Stack Square and the nearby Shepherd's Square were still intact and ideal for their purpose. Discussions were even held with the National Coal Board regarding the possible removal or screening of the high voltage overhead supply lines which crossed the site.

Blaenafon Town Council had been planning to demolish the ruins of the ironworks and also Stack Square, as part of a slum clearance programme, but they now agreed that these buildings should be retained for use in the proposed film. Undoubtedly, it would bring large numbers of visitors to the town and provide a welcome source of much needed revenue.

The following year it was announced by Stanley Baker that his Oakhurst Company had acquired a film script of *Rape of the Fair Country* and that he intended to make the film in Blaenafon with extensive use of local people as extras.

Sadly, the necessary finance was not forthcoming and none of these proposals came to fruition despite the fact that this exciting novel has all the ingredients to make a very moving and dramatic blockbuster.

By 1985 the film had still not been made and Cordell observed: "For twelve years the talk of making a film of the book was up and down like a yo-yo and more would-be producers' hearts were broken on it than the epic *Ben Hur*. Eventually, I stopped believing that it would ever happen. I would only be convinced when I was standing in the queue at the box office."

A CONVERSATION WITH ALEXANDER CORDELL

One day in September 1987, I recorded Alexander Cordell's memories of the period when he was undertaking research for *Rape of the Fair Country*. Our conversation began whilst we were sitting on a bench, enjoying a flask of coffee, at the site of Capel Newydd, just outside Blaenafon.

I first asked Alex, "How long did you spend on the background research for *Rape of the Fair Country* ?"

He replied, "It was carried out over a period of about two and a half years and I travelled around the area on a little autocycle which I had bought for the grand sum of £10. As I rode around, I would stop every man and woman who I judged to be over the age of seventy and ask them about their memories of the *old days*.

The more I travelled around this locality and researched in libraries, it became clear to me that there was a fascinating story to be told of the people who lived and worked here during the grim times of the Industrial Revolution. I have very special memories of afternoons and evenings spent sipping tea by cottage fire-sides, talking to the old folk of Blaenafon. People who tolerated the questions of a total stranger, opened their doors to me and gave me such kind hospitality. How well I remember the two old men who gave me tots of whisky in a little back room of a terraced cottage in North Street, and racked their brains trying to remember what their grandfathers had told them.

My on the spot research was supplemented by ten days hard graft at the National Library of Wales in Aberystwyth and this utterly confirmed so many of the grim stories of hardship and exploitation that I had been told. I had started my research unbiased, and wishing to be the champion of only one cause - to tell the story of the people who left a heritage - a people who laid the foundations of a great industry. But before long I had become an angry young man, consumed with passion for the exploited workers and burning with anger against the ruthless ironmasters."

"Was there any particular experience that initially inspired you to write the novel," I asked.

"Yes, it was during the afternoon that I first travelled up the mountain road from Abergavenny, over the side of the Blorenge towards Blaenafon and stumbled across Garnddyrys. The deserted *Victoria* Inn was still standing then. Locked and barred it seemed to be guarded by sheep. Nearby was a row of roofless cottages and as I took in the glorious view, I began to think of the people who once lived in that windswept spot.

Following a track down below the road, I found the tramroad and then climbed to the top of the old furnace tips, all the time wondering about the events that once took place on this scarred hillside. I stood before the rusted grates of tumble-down cottages; touched scraps of faded wallpaper and tried to recapture the laughter and tears of a village that had died; the clang of the pots on ovens, the scrape of hobnails, quarrellings and whispered love. I realised that here on this hillside was the story of a people who were now but dust, but by courage and labour had built an industry, which had now also vanished. The village was called Garnddyrys and it was once a thriving community, a little town of people who lived their lives on the edge of a golden valley."

Remains of ironworkers' cottages at Garnddyrys

"I was so excited after my first visit to Garndyrys that I must have clocked 50 miles an hour on my journey down the mountain, heading back to my cottage in Llanelen. In bed that night, I tossed and turned longing for someone to tell me a story. A young lady called Morfydd entered my thoughts and introduced me to her brother aged seven. His name was Iestyn Mortymer, though I never knew why.

The following day was a Saturday, and again I do not know why, but I made my way to Nantyglo, pedalling up the Black Rock pitch like something demented, past the desolation of the Clydach Gorge to reach the old furnace tips above Cwm Crachen. I remember being fascinated by the topsy-turvy houses and the gaunt remains of old workings. Sitting on a pile of slag I sat and pondered on the scene before me.

I then made my way down into Nantyglo and fell into conversation with a Mr Jenkins, who told me about the old iron-making that laid the foundation of greatness that Wales enjoys today, and I left this man inspired.

He was just one of scores of such men that I met in later years, ranging from town clerks to invalid miners. They instilled in me the will to write what was, for me, the greatest theme I had ever discovered. I knew now that, hand in hand with the pioneer ironmasters went the fight of the Welsh for a standard of decency during the degrading, early years of the Industrial Revolution.

In Nantyglo, I visited the *Royal Oak Inn* where arms were handed out by Zephaniah Williams for the Chartist attack on Newport, and then travelled on to Blackwood to see the *Coach and Horses Inn*, which was John Frost's headquarters at the time of the riot.

I later spent time in council offices perusing records, met and talked with men on street corners, sometimes retired overmen living out their drab lives in small back rooms. Walking the mountains, I chatted to lonely men, who raked the dim recesses of their minds for what their fathers had told them. I was given tea in cottages, never turned away from any door, never rejected.

Photography played a part too, for I took hundreds of photographs of old workings and cinder-tips, tram roads, balance ponds, workers' cottages and lonely chapels.

Writing the book, chiefly in the evenings, I spent my weekends in interviews, visiting churchyards and graves, noting their sad epitaphs. And the more I delved into the history of South Wales, the more evident became my realisation that behind the drive of the early pioneers of the Industrial Revolution lay the moving story of a people who had been sacrificed for the attainment of personal fortunes."

Having finished our coffee we then drove back to Blaenafon and made our way to the old ironworks to see how the restoration work was progressing. Standing in front of Stack Square, we gazed in companionable silence for a moment, across the valley and then Alex remarked, "Before any industry came here this valley would have been quite unspoilt and all we would have seen from this spot would have been small farmsteads dotted here and there. But by the nineteenth century this valley would have been alive with the sounds of industry and it is said the glare from the furnaces was so strong that you could read the small print of a newspaper quite easily at midnight."

"Living at Stack Square when the furnaces were in operation must have been very unpleasant," I commented.

"I quite agree," said Alex. "But just think, they could tumble out of bed and go straight on shift. The beds of course never got a chance to get cold, for as one lodger went off to work another man came in on finishing his shift."

William Byrne's engraving of Blaenafon Ironworks based on Sir Richard Colt Hoare's drawing made in 1799, and published in William Coxe's *An Historical Tour of Monmouthshire* in 1801

I then recalled my own delvings into Blaenafon's past, "The 1851 Census records that 84 people lived in Stack Square and it seems amazing now, but as many as ten people sometimes lived in one of these small cottages and one couple even raised as many as nineteen children here!"

"Yes, I remember reading that in my own research," said Alex, "and the people of course all had to do their shopping in the nearby Company shop, where anything from a pin to a shroud was sold. Pay day was every six weeks and the ironmasters' agents paid the men in the *Drum and Monkey Inn* which was situated in North Street. Apparently, the paymasters would often wait until the men were too drunk to count their wages and they would go home sometimes with seven quarts of ale inside them and hardly any money for their wives. Of course they didn't all do this, but some certainly did. They were paid in tokens which could only be spent in the Company shop.

The prices at these shops were often thirty per cent higher than that of goods offered by private enterprise, which was naturally discouraged if not banned. As a result, the early ironworkers found themselves tied body and soul to masters who offered them the alternative of acceptance of the Truck system or starvation.

However, I must say that the workers of Blaenafon and Garnddyrys were more fortunate than those of most iron towns along the Heads of the Valleys. Their lives were undoubtedly influenced by the Christianity of Samuel Hopkins and his sister Sarah, who generally had their workers' interests at heart."

Below the ironworks, Alex showed me where Shepherd Square (demolished in 1964) had once stood. It was in one of these terraced cottages that he had placed his Mortymer family. Situated at the south end of Staffordshire Row it was similar in layout to Stack Square with the cottages built on three sides of a courtyard.

"It is most unfortunate that these houses were demolished, for as the home of the fictitious Mortymer family, they would have undoubtedly proved a popular tourist attraction," I remarked.

"Yes," said Alex. "Visitors would certainly have found the cottages interesting and they could have been furnished in the style of the 1830s, just like they do with the buildings at St Fagans. In my novel the Mortymer family represented the Welsh respectability of that period. Hywel Mortymer, the father depicted the manhood of Wales; and Eleanor was a Welsh mother whose arms embraced the whole family. Iestyn, and his

The Rolling Mill in Broad Street was where Alexander Cordell began a series of interviews with local people which led to him writing *Rape of the Fair Country*

Shepherd's Square, demolished in 1964, was where Cordell placed his fictitious Mortymer family

sister Morfydd stood for the new generation who revolted at the impossible social conditions.

Hywel, or Dada as I sometimes call him, was larger than life and I portrayed him as the father that I always wanted to have had and he was also the man that I always wanted to be."

It was pointless looking for the old *Drum and Monkey Inn*, for that had long since disappeared, along with a large number of Blaenafon's other public houses. At one time local men would have been able to boast that it was possible to drink in a different pub every week in the year in Blaenafon!

Alex commented, "Not every head of a family found solace in drink. In the respectable homes, the closing of the cottage door after shift meant security; the ironworker's home was a castle with curtains to shut out the furnace glare. Many of the people were of course deeply religious and within the covers of the Bible they found a contentment that was far removed from the rushed anxieties of today. Visiting preachers travelled these valleys, bringing further spiritual uplift. Local preachers, usually self-appointed were fervent in their beliefs that the new era of industry was a period of trial from which Wales and Welshmen would emerge triumphant. And as depravity spread deeper into the rowdies so the God-fearing classes adhered more strongly to the code that was a passport to Heaven. The churches were full every Sunday. Hymns were sung to the harp, open-air religious meetings were thickly attended.

Music and processions also played an important part in the lives of these people. From their meagre wage-packets, they saved pennies to buy brass instruments. Bands were formed which competed under strict adjudicators. These bands had their headquarters in the tap-rooms of the inns and taverns and they all had their respective colours. On Benefit night most of the population would turn out for the annual procession."

We had now arrived at St Peter's Church and I commented that in *Rape of the Fair Country* it was here that Iestyn and Mari were married.

Alex said, "Yes that is right, I did not give his name in the book, but they would have been married by the Rev James Jenkins who was the first vicar when the church opened in 1805 and he remained here until his retirement thirty seven years later. I remember reading that in one of his sermons one Sunday evening, he took for his text the words: 'Two women shall be grinding at the mill, the one shall be taken and the other left.'

The *Whistle Inn* is where Iestyn stoped for a pint of beer "to settle the dust" on his way to his wedding to Mari Dirion at St Peter's Church, Blaenafon.

St Peter's Church was built by the ironmasters Thomas Hill and Samuel Hopkins at their own expense in 1804

"At this point the entire congregation lost control of itself, with people standing up and weeping loudly. The sermon was of sad significance to them for it referred to a recent brickyard accident in which a young woman was helping another in supplying a mill with clay. The clothes of the woman caught in the cogs of the machinery and she was pulled through the rollers and badly mangled."

I commented, " Accidents must have occurred very frequently in those times when labour was cheap and plentiful and there were certainly no health and safety at work regulations as there are today."

Alex nodded and replied, "Yes unskilled labour, poor technicians and the employment of young children must have contributed to the dangers of the early furnaces, which were far from safe by modern standards. There was also the extensive network of tramroads, often passing above precipitous heights and through such dangerous places as the Pwll-du to Blaenavon tunnel. All these would have produced a large accident rate. Puddling and firebox work also caused many casualties through blindness.

One of the most tragic accidents, in the period we are talking about, involved a mining disaster at the Cinder Pit, which cost the lives of fourteen men and two women. The Afon Lwyd overflowed and ran down a horse drift into the pit drowning those working below. During the rescue operations, eight of the bodies were found clinging to each other, but all were recovered and decently buried."

We had now reached the derelict St Peter's School which was the first school in Wales to be established by an ironmaster for the benefit of the workers' children. It was sad to see this historic building in such a poor state of repair and we both agreed that it was important that it should be preserved, and a suitable use found for it.

Alex recalled, "The first recognised school in Blaenafon was opened at Bunker's Row by Samuel Hopkins in 1814 and he engaged a workman's wife to teach the children. Two other schools followed in rapid succession, at the little Quick Building and at Capel-y-graig. It was no doubt this fine man's intention to establish a solid educational system in Blaenafon, but unfortunately he died in June 1815. However, his good sister Sarah, then took it upon herself to build a lasting memorial to the work of her brother, and, at her own expense, erected and founded in 1816 the Endowed schools that remained in use over a century and a half later. She also formulated an educational curriculum, engaged teachers and even herself assisted in the teaching.

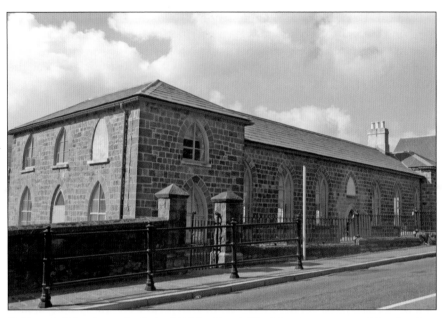

St Peter's School was built in 1816 by Sarah Hopkins in memory of her brother Samuel. It is now a Visitor Centre for the Blaenafon World Heritage Site.

"Few of the local people at this time could read or write and their simple attitude to life was largely based on myth and legend. They were very superstitious and many even believed in fairies. Elgam Farm for instance, was believed to house the tylwyth teg (fairies) and people in Cae White cottages, the Brickyard cottages and Bunker's Row would not dare cross the road after dark for fear of the *Little Folk*. "

We passed the impressive Workmen's Hall and then turned up Broad Street, which is the main shopping area of the town. Alex commented on how run down the town was starting to look and recalled that it had been so much busier and more alive when he was walking these same streets in 1957, whilst researching his novel. He told me how some of his first interviews with local people had been carried out in the *Rolling Mill*, a pub once popular with colliers and ironworkers. Over pints of beer, he had gathered some fascinating material and it was here for example, that he was told stories of prize fighting which used to take place quite regularly in the Punchbowl, a remote hollow, on the north side of the Blorenge mountain.

"On Sunday mornings when the deacons were in chapel, fighters came from the neighbouring towns to pit their skill and strength against the pugilists of Garnddyrys and Blaenafon. The contests were bare-knuckled and brutal with Queensbury Rules rarely applied. The art of self-defence was taught down the generations, and as soon as a boy approached working age he was instructed by his father.

I remember a local collier mentioning Jem Mace, who was once the Champion of England, but he could thank his lucky stars that he had never set foot in Wales, for five out of six of the hard drinkers of the *Drum and Monkey* would have seen him off to burial without the help of a service!"

"They were certainly brutal times," I commented, "and hooliganism must have been rife in this mountain town during the time that your novel was set."

Alex nodded and said, "The most terrifying violence of course was handed out by the Scotch Cattle, men who took secret oaths and banded together to force the rest of the community to their will. The leader of such a band was called 'The Bull.' He was selected for his strength and cruelty and dressing himself in skins, he adorned his head with the horns of a cow or bull.

The Scotch Cattle made night attacks on the houses of black legs during times of strikes. They painted the head of a bull in red on the door of the black leg's house and if this warning did not persuade the man to strike, then they returned to ransack the house, burn the furniture and the man was flogged. If you remember this happened to Hywel Mortymer in my novel.

It must be remembered that the advent of the Scotch Cattle was a direct outcome of the desperate conditions of the times and these bands of men were hated by masters and workers alike. Military assistance from Brecon Garrison was even enlisted by the masters to put them down.

Opposing the Scotch Cattle and their brutal methods of enforcing total strike were the Chartists. They were the idealists; men driven to leadership by the conditions of labour and living. But, I must say that Chartism was not strong here in Blaenafon; for conditions here were not as bad, by comparison with those of the other Iron Towns at the heads of the valleys. In Nantyglo, for example, Chartism thrived largely because Crawshay Bailey, the Nantyglo ironmaster, ground the last ounce from his workers and had little interest in their spiritual or physical welfare. It is also significant that it was in the adjoining town of Coalbrookvale (now Blaina) that Zephaniah Williams, the landlord of the *Royal Oak Inn*, made his Chartist headquarters.

Probably the man who influenced the Monmouthshire Chartists as a whole was William Lovett, who advocated peaceful settlement of social grievances. But as the plans for violence increased so Lovett's stock diminished.

At the time of the unsuccessful and tragic rising of Sunday, November 3rd 1839 the Blaenafon contingent which is said to have 'returned in soaked misery,' were dispirited, I guess, not half so much by the weather as by their disbelief in violence. Under Lovett's influence they could hardly be named as extremists and in a town where a man was transported for the theft of a Bible, much can be said for the moderation of their views."

By now we had reached the new car park at the Ironworks and to shelter from the pouring rain which had suddenly hit the town, we sat inside my car. I then asked Alex how his career as a writer had first started.

"In the beginning I started writing short stories and my first one was about a deep sea diver. On showing it to my mother, she suggested that I sent it off to a woman's magazine called *Red Letter*. They paid well and I was encouraged to write further short stories. My first book was written much later and it was autobiographical, being based on my wartime experience. I wrote it because I just had to get my hatred of the war out of my system. Sadly, when the novel was first published in 1954 it was not particularly successful. It sold much better when it was re-published under a different title some years later, after I had become established as an author through the success of *Rape of the Fair Country*.

I first realised that I could write about Wales when I was living in Llanelen, and that of course is where I first started writing *Rape of the Fair Country* . In order to develop a writer's ear for the speech of the Valleys Welsh, I used to go to Abergavenny Market and listen to the women who had come down from places like Blaenafon and Brynmawr and try to tune in to their lilting musical accents. Their conversations were generally lively, even bawdy at times and I felt inspired. In that way I tried to envisage how the Welsh spoke in the time of which I would be writing."

"What advice would you give to anyone who is starting to write their first novel," I asked.

"To write successfully, you have to write about what you know and feel. The three ingredients for writing any novel, to my mind, are sincerity, simplicity and humility. I remember the well known Welsh author Jack Jones once saying to me, after the publication of *Rape of the Fair Country*,

'Any one who writes a book about Wales had better be sure of his facts, for he is asking for trouble if they are wrong.' Generally, I spend at least eighteen months carrying out research before writing any novel. The actual writing part may only take six months. My facts are all based on thorough research into local histories, public health records, company records; in fact anything which relates to the period."

I then commented,"It must have been a great disappointment to you that the proposed film of *Rape of the Fair Country* has never been made. It seems amazing to me that no producer has yet emerged with the will and the financial backing to take on such a worthwhile project. To my mind it has all the ingredients to make a very successful feature film, that would do wonders for tourism in Wales."

Alex replied, "I have no doubt that it will be made after I have gone and that the script writers and the director will manage to alter my story beyond recognition. They will hopefully film it during your time, but surely not in mine."

"Well," I said, "I am sure that you are right and that it will be done one day. You have my assurance that I will certainly do my best to cause it to be made if I possibly can."

Alexander Cordell at the site of Capel Newydd in 1985

BACKGROUND TO THE CHARTISTS' UPRISING

The climax to *Rape of the Fair Country* is the story of the Chartists' uprising and the march on Newport in 1839. Alexander Cordell was the first novelist to feature this historic event and he has ensured that it will never be forgotten.

It was undoubtedly the Truck Act that accelerated the Chartists' movement in Monmouthshire because it was a poisonous thorn in the lives of coal and ironworkers and caused very bad feeling between masters and men after 1800. The ironmasters and colliery owners had opened provision shops adjoining their works at which the men obtained commodities instead of wages.

The employers exploited the workers by charging high prices beyond the earning capacity of the men, who often had large families to keep. These shops became a primary source of unrest and the whole truck system was condemned as cruel and oppressive. The labouring masses were being denied the genuine social privilege of spending their wages as they wished.

In June 1829, the evils of the Truck Act were discussed at Pontypool Law Sessions and this was a preliminary to a joint petition to Parliament by Monmouthshire magistrates to remove the hated shops. Refusal of a miner to deal in his employer's shop meant immediate dismissal. John Frost, who had become the champion of the working classes in Newport by 1830, addressed a mass meeting there in 1831. He prophesied the 1839 rebellion and the years of suffering ahead of them, and referred to the opposing interests of governors and industrial workers to retain power on the one hand and freedom on the other.

"The poor workmen are compelled to call at the 'Tommy Shops'. If the shop manager gave away cash in exchange for vouchers, the money was never taken out but transferred to the customers' account with the shop. This is the shameful course now adopted by the Pharoah-like ironmasters to screen themselves from the penalties of the law in withholding from their half-starved labourers their hard earnings."

Monmouthshire Merlin 10th March 1832

Many Government Courts of Enquiry were set up to investigate the effects of the Truck Acts in Monmouthshire and elsewhere, but little would be done until the Trade Unions inspired by the Chartist revolt of 1839 became strong enough to apply retaliatory measures with their own co-operative stores.

It was in this extreme state of unrest and embitterment that John Frost and his confederates were able to lead a strong agitation against a capitalist monopoly that caused a sense of serfdom and oppression. The Chartist movement no doubt received its inspiration from the French Revolution, when the Charter of Liberties secured the freedom of the French nation.

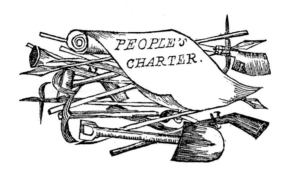

The People's Charter of 1836 had been drawn up by the London Working Men's Association as a result of the working classes becoming disillusioned by the Reform Act of 1832 which had promised them greater parliamentary representation.

The population of the mining valleys of Monmouthshire were not represented in Parliament and this further inflamed the workers' passions and filled them with suspicion of political reformers. Frost's influence grew in Newport and also in the county, where he had worthy partners in William Jones and Zephaniah Williams. In the West of England the Chartist movement was focused on Bristol and as both Jones and Frost were Bristol born, they had many relatives and friends in that city to supply them with information on the latest developments in the national Chartist organisation.

The document known as the 'Peoples' Charter' was drawn up in 1838 and prepared as a Parliamentary Bill by William Lovett, the Secretary of the London Working Mens' Association, and Francis Place who was a London tailor. Their charter contained six points:-

1. Universal Suffrage
2. Equal Electoral Districts
3. Annual Parliaments
4. Vote by Ballot
5. Abolition of the Property Qualification for election to Parliament
6. Payment of Members of Parliament

The Chartists' national newspaper was the *Northern Star* which was published in Leeds and distributed all over Britain, but there were not many working people of this period who could read. In Monmouthshire, the followers of Chartism read the *Western Vindicator* and took their inspiration from the fiery writings of Henry Vincent. It is on record that the ironmaster Crawshay Bailey actually sacked three of his workmen for reading this paper which is some indication of the concern felt by the ironmasters at this time, for it must have been obvious to them that the Chartist movement was growing in strength week by week.

John Frost

John Frost was the son of John and Sarah Frost, who kept the *Royal Oak* Public House in Thomas Street, Newport. Born on May 25th 1784, he was raised by grandparents, following the death of his father.

At the age of sixteen he was apprenticed to a Cardiff tailor, but by about 1816 he was back in Newport running his own business. He married the widow of Mr Geech, a timber merchant, by whom he had two sons and five daughters.

A few years later a quarrel took place between John Frost and Thomas Prothero. The cause of it was an action in which Prothero was professionally engaged against a relative of Frost, who had himself become security for the payment. Prothero having succeeded in his action, Frost was forced to make a payment of the sum for which he was responsible.

Conceiving himself injured by proceedings which had been ruinous to his business Frost threatened to lay the whole case before the public unless the sum he had been obliged to pay was refunded.

This threat was considered an attempt to extort money and it resulted in a prosecution. Frost had to sell off all his stock to pay his creditors with the exception of one of his relatives who claimed a debt of £200. In 1822 he suffered six months' imprisonment for libel upon Prothero and was incarcerated in Cold Bath Field's Prison, Monmouth.

On his return to Newport, after his release from prison, he was regarded as a popular hero and his entry into the town resembled a triumphal procession with flags flying and shouts of congratulation. From this time he left his shop to the care of his family and his undivided energies were devoted to politics.

He led a strong anti-Morgan feeling in Newport after 1832, because Thomas Prothero, the agent of the Morgan Estates, refused to grant trading facilities to the Workmen's Societies in coal and other commodities. These workmen's clubs were prominent in the valleys of Monmouthshire and were secret concerns aiming at the workers' welfare and social freedom.

Frost won a seat on the Newport Town Council and became Mayor of the Borough in 1836, but got into hot water for criticising his fellow members and the town clerk. His hopes of being re-elected Mayor in 1837 were frustrated and his conduct as Mayor was a subject of special investigation. This infuriated Frost, especially when his deadliest opponent on the council, Thomas Phillips, the former town clerk, was elected Mayor in his stead.

On New Year's Day in 1839, a meeting of 7,000 members of the Working Mens' Association at Pontnewynydd heard John Frost denounce the financial extravagance of the government, in particular the £1,000 a year paid to each of the Queen's twelve grooms of the bed chamber.

Frost was chosen by the gathering of the Pontypool delegates to represent the Monmouthshire Chartists at the meeting of the National Convention of the Industrious Classes on the 4th February 1839.

His speech at Pontypool however, earned him a warning from Lord Russell, the Home Secretary, that a continuance of such conduct "would result in his name being erased from the Commision of the Peace for the County of Monmouth."

To this warning, Frost replied with a violent denial of the Home Secretary's right to interfere with his freedom of speech or opinion and continued his agitation at public meetings held throughout the county. Lord Russell then carried out his threat and Frost's name was struck from the roll of magistrates.

In early 1839 the workers were fired with a new determination to cast off the fetters of bondage, and Frost and his colleagues wrote vehement articles in the press advocating the Chartist demands as their Charter of Liberty from capitalist domination and ruthless suppression.

On May 3rd 1839, the Government stopped all armed assemblies and four days later, the People's Petition, bearing 1,200,000 names, was left tamely at the House of Commons to be presented some other day.

Henry Vincent was arrested on May 10th in London, lodged in Monmouth prison and was almost the subject of a rescue by the miners until John Frost came hurriedly to control these men.

Matters came to a head on October 27th when large numbers of Chartists met at the *Coach and Horses Inn*, Blackwood. Plans were made for a march on Newport. Three columns from the valleys - from West Monmouthshire led by John Frost, from Nantyglo led by Zephaniah Williams, and William Jones's column from Pontypool - were to meet on the outskirts of Newport, to arrive in the town at 2 am, and wreck the Usk Bridge.

THE MARCH ON NEWPORT

It was at the *Coach and Horses* in Blackwood that the plans were made for the big march on Newport. The assembled delegates resolved that all lodge members should meet, fully armed at several vantage points on the evening of Sunday 3rd November. They would then march in three separate divisions towards Newport.

The *Coach and Horses Inn*, Blackwood (now demolished)

The western division would advance from Blackwood and be led by John Frost himself. Zephaniah Williams would gather together his followers near Nantyglo and the third contingent led by William Jones would march from Pontypool. In due course the three groups would join forces in the vicinity of Cefn on the outskirts of Newport and then march as one body into the town, arriving at 2.00 a.m., when the inhabitants would be sound asleep and completely unaware of their presence. They would first overpower the soldiers and then demolish the bridge over the Usk and hold up the mail coach from Birmingham. The non-arrival of letters from Wales in that city was to be regarded as a signal for insurrection to commence. After taking control of Newport a detachment would then march to Monmouth Gaol to release Henry Vincent and his fellow prisoners.

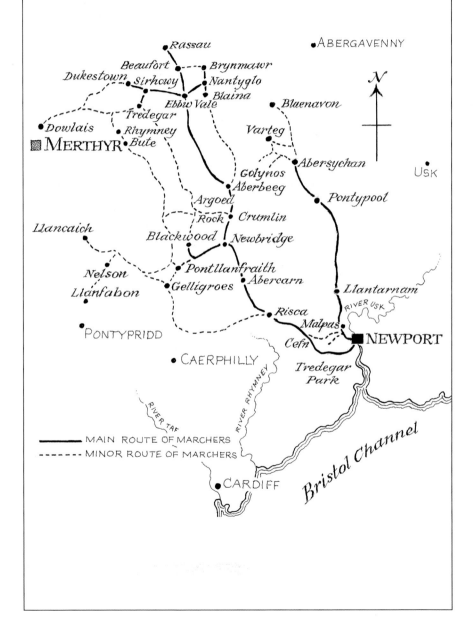

ROUTES TAKEN BY CHARTIST MARCHERS

MAIN ROUTE OF MARCHERS

MINOR ROUTE OF MARCHERS

A man came to the *Coach and Horses* at about 7.00 pm and informed John Frost that he had come from Newport, that the soldiers there were all Chartists, that their arms and ammunition were packed up, and that they were ready to join the Chartists as soon as they arrived. There was of course no foundation for this statement!

On November 3rd 1839, men from Tredegar and Sirhowy marched down the valley to join John Frost at Blackwood. The previous day 300 men had walked from Merthyr and Dowlais to join the Tredegar group and one of them was William Griffiths of Merthyr who was subsequently killed outside the Westgate Hotel.

John Frost placed himself at the head of his band of men and shouted "Follow me," and they set forth along the tramroad through Pentwyn Mawr. They called at various public houses on the way and then passed through Newbridge. Men were sent into numerous houses during the march to persuade others to join them. But in most cases the male occupants had already left their homes and hidden in nearby woods and other places to avoid being drawn into the march by force. They marched on through Abercarn and Risca.

> "O! ye who love glory, we heed not the story
> Of Waterloo won with the blood of the brave
> But we dare the rough storm, in the cause of reform
> Then let the red banner triumphantly wave,"

Welsh Chartist song 1839

The Western Valley Chartists

Zephaniah Williams was the leader of the Western Valley contingent of the Chartist supporters and he kept the old *Royal Oak Inn* at Coalbrookvale. He was born in Argoed in the Sirhowy Valley in 1795, the son of a local farmer, and received a good education in Welsh and English. He became a mining engineer and in 1828 was appointed as the mineral agent at the Sirhowy Ironworks, Tredegar. In 1839 he moved from his home at Dukestown to become the innkeeper of the *Royal Oak Inn* at Coalbrookvale.

It is said that prior to the Chartist march on Newport, there were 1,500 pikes and a large collection of guns and pistols hidden in the cellars of the *Royal Oak*. The supporters mainly came from the Coalbrookvale Ironworks which was owned by the Brewers and also from the Cwmcelyn Works of the Brown family. By mid-839, membership of the Ebbw Fach Association had risen to 750.

The Brynmawr Lodge met at the beershop home of 37 year old David Lewis who was the landlord of the *King Crispin*, in Boundary Street, Brynmawr, and he also worked as a shoemaker.

Zephaniah Williams

In the Nantyglo area during the day before the march, orders were being passed to the Chartist supporters, to meet with Zephaniah Williams on the mountain between Nantyglo and Ebbw Vale. They were told to bring supplies of bread and cheese for they would be away from home for some time. It was also strongly inferred that if they did not attend the meeting then their lives would be in danger.

Many of the men first went to the *Royal Oak Inn* where they were supplied with weapons from the lodge-room. Guns and swords were not numerous, but there were many pikes available, which had been specially forged for the purpose. Additional weapons were improvised by fastening knifes to the ends of sticks.

Groups of men began to assemble at Bwlch y Garn on the hillside above Nantyglo at just after 5.00 p.m. and eventually between four and five thousand men were there, all armed with a wide assortment of weapons.

Zephaniah Williams dramatically mounted a convenient tump to address his followers who stood there waiting in anticipation in the driving rain and the cutting wind. His speech was short for he was not a man to waste words, "My dear Chartists, you need not be frightened, because we are bound to be in Newport by two o' clock. The soldiers will not touch you."

The mass of men then raised their weapons and shouted in unison, "We don't care for them!" Zephaniah then finished his oration with a brief command in Welsh, "Dewch ymlaen fechgyn!" - "Come on boys!"

He then stepped down from the mound and placed himself at the head of the party to begin the march to Newport. The men were by now thankful to be on the move, for many of them had been exposed to the elements on that bleak hillside for over two hours and drenched to the skin, they were shivering with the cold.

Zephaniah Williams kept going backwards and forwards along the line of marchers, telling the men that they were going down to Newport to show the people that they were determined to get the Charter made the law of the land. They would be there by two o' clock in the morning and there would be no shedding of blood.

They moved down from the mountain into the Ebbw Fawr Valley and in spite of Zephaniah's injunctions many were in a riotous mood. On reaching the tramway at the foot of the mountain near Cwm, a short halt was made to gather the forces together and then they marched on towards Risca. On the way they stopped at various inns, but by 11.00 p.m. they had reached the *Coach and Horses* at Llanhilleth which was about fifteen miles from Newport. The landlord was woken up by a loud banging on the door and he came downstairs to find a dozen men standing outside, demanding refreshments. In fear of his life he served them and when they had departed, he returned to his bed. However a few moments later another, much larger party arrived. When he opened the door, they rushed inside and he must have wondered what on earth was happening.

It was 1.30 a.m. before Zephaniah Williams himself reached the *Coach and Horses* and by now his men had all marched on ahead of him towards Newport. He sat down inside the inn by the fire and his sodden clothes steamed as he downed his quart of ale. The landlord was persuaded to provide a horse and trap in which Zephaniah and a few friends were driven down the valley to Ty'n-y-cwm Farm where they arrived at about 7.00 a.m. *The Welsh Oak* at Rogerstone was now just a short distance away, where the rest of the marchers should be waiting.

The Welsh Oak was a major rallying point for the marching Chartists and it was just four miles from Newport. John Frost's contingent had arrived here at about 2.00 a.m. and were awaiting the arrival of the group led by Zephaniah Williams of Nantyglo.

The landlord was Henry Charles, and soon his small inn was bulging to the seams with thirsty marchers. Others, realising that it would be impossible for them to get a drink there, continued to Cefn to quench their thirst at another public house.

Thomas Saunders, a farmer who lived near the *The Welsh Oak*, heard a noise on the tramway outside his house at midnight just after he had retired to bed. He decided that it was probably some people being rather merry at the public house and he put his head back on the pillow. However, a few moments later, he heard someone calling him by name, so he went to his bedroom window and shouted, "What do you want at this time of night?" "Get up quickly and come down here, and I will tell you," came the reply. Saunders then hurriedly dressed and went downstairs where his friend told him, "You had better hide for there are thousands of Chartists on the tramroad."

Now, very alarmed, Saunders rushed away and hid among the straw in his barn. It was not long before a group of Chartists opened the door of the barn and came inside to shelter from the driving rain. Saunders then began

The *Welsh Oak Inn* at Rogerstone

The *Welsh Oak* at Rogerstone takes its name from the Golynos Oak which once stood in this locality. It was said to be the largest oak tree in Britain and when felled in 1810 it yielded 2,426 feet of timber. The diameter of the trunk was just over 9 feet.

to worry about the safety of his home so he crept out of the barn and returned to his house, which he found full of Chartists warming themselves in front of a fire they had lit. Having satisfied himself that his house had not been damaged, Saunders then began to worry about his barn, fearing that the sheltering men might set it on fire. So he went back to the barn and asked them to take care with their candles. He then returned to the house again and found the Chartists trying to dry their clothes in front of the fire.

Meanwhile, Zephaniah Williams had finally arrived at the *Welsh Oak Inn* and he and John Frost were making an attempt to arrange their followers into some sort of order. Eventually they decided to march on to Newport. Frost commanded those who had guns to go to the front, those who possessed pikes were to go next, followed by men armed with bludgeons. Those who had no arms at all were told to follow in the rear.

The Eastern Valley Chartists

On Sunday 3rd November a large meeting had been held at the *Bristol Beerhouse* in Pontypool which was the residence of William Jones, leader of the Eastern Valley contingent. The men came as instructed, armed with guns, pikes and any other weapons that they could procure. Those who arrived without weapons were told to go to a house at the top of Trosnant Street, where they could obtain guns, swords and pistols.

They were told to muster that evening at the Race and by 10.00 p.m. a large crowd had gathered despite the appalling weather. Jones shouted through the wind and explained that the people of Newport were expecting their arrival in three bodies, and it was essential for them to be prompt.

Just as he was finishing his speech, a contingent led by a beerhouse keeper, John Llewellyn, arrived from Pontnewynydd. Many of the men had no doubt come to the meeting merely out of curiosity and intended to just make their way home at the end of it. But this proved very difficult, for the armed men had been stationed at various points to prevent the escape of any such deserters.

At 11.00 p.m. they began the march to Newport, with men, five abreast, carrying firearms in the front, followed by those who had spears and the rest followed behind.

Numerous houses were broken into on the way and the male inhabitants forced to join their ranks. At about 4.00 a.m the main body passed through Pontypool and stopped outside the Station house. Then considered attacking it to release the prisoners inside, but thought better of it and decided to press on instead to the *Upper Cock Inn* at Croes-y-celiog. Large numbers of men, now drenched and ravenous, made their way inside. Others spent their time in the vicinity of Croes-y-celiog going from house to house to persuade by threats and force every man they could find to join the march.

William Jones

William Jones at 6.00 a.m. gave a sword and dagger to his lieutenant and sent him forward to lead the main party of men, whilst he remained behind to bring together the stragglers. Many were by now dragging their feet and Jones persuaded them to continue by pointing a pistol at their heads and threatening to blow out their brains if they did not obey him.

> "The labourer toils and strives the more
>   While Tyrants are carousing
>   But Hark! I hear the lions roar,
>   Our British youth is rousing,
>   The rich are liable to pain.
>   The poor man feels the smart, Sir,
>   So let us break the despot's chain,
>   We soon will have the Charter.

The advance guard which numbered between 2,000 and 3,000 men, reached the *Green House* (*Y Ty Gwyrdd*) at Llantarnam where another stop was made to quench their seemingly insatiable thirst.

On hearing of their arrival, Mr. Blewitt, MP, who lived at Llantarnam Abbey, came out to talk to them and emphasised that, "certain ruin awaited them if they set themselves against the authorities of the country." But the marching men ignored him and pressed on towards Newport.

When they reached Malpas Court about one hundred and fifty men entered the stable yard and compelled the gardener and coachman to fall in with the marchers. Then on they went to the Marshes Turnpike Gate on the outskirts of Newport, where they positioned a few men with orders to direct following marchers up the lane (now known as Barrack Hill) towards Penylan.

It was 10.00 a.m. when William Jones arrived here to join his men and they were suddenly surprised to see other men rushing in large numbers from the direction of Newport. Jones grabbed one of them and asked him what had hapenned in Newport. Breathlessly, the man, obviously frightened and very weary, told him that an attack had been made on the *Westgate Hotel*...three or four men had been killed and the whole body were defeated. Jones apparently then exclaimed "Oh! damn me; then we are done!"

The news soon spread from man to man and before long they were all making their way homewards as fast as they possibly could. The motley army of William Jones the Watchmaker scattered like leaves blown in the wind.

Onwards to the Westgate Inn

John Frost's party had left the *Welsh Oak* and followed the Turnpike Road to Ty Du, then via the *Globe Beer House*, Tre Gwillim and Pye Corner where stops were made for further refreshment at the *Three Horseshoes Inn* and the *Pine Apple Beer House*. The men who stopped however were soon ordered out by one of the Chartist captains.

From there the marchers followed the tramroad through Tredegar Park, which was owned by Sir Charles Morgan, and at 8.00 a.m. they halted at the Cwrt y Bella weighing machine which was about one mile from the centre of Newport. Climbing Bell Vue Lane they went past a large house known as the Friars to reach the turnpike gate on Stow Hill.

The marchers made their way up Waterloo Road and Friars Road to pass the large Gothic style house known as the Friars. At the time it was being reconstructed on the site of a much older building.

WESTGATE HOTEL

19th century engraving of the Chartists storming the *Westgate Hotel*, Newport,

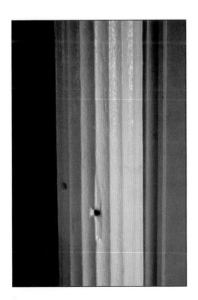

Hollow wooden pillars at the entrance to the old Westgate Hotel reputed to be perforated by the Chartists' bullets

The Chartist Tower overlooking John Frost Square commemorates the Chartist who died in the uprising of November 1839

The Chartist Song

Then rouse my boys and fight the foe
Your weapons are truth and reason
We will let the Whigs and Tories know
That thinking is not treason

Ye Lords oppose us if you can
Your own doom you seek after
With or without you we will stand
Until we gain the Charter

Chorus
Despair shall no longer our spirits dismay
Nor wither the arm when upraised for the fray
The conflict for feedom is gathering nigh
We live to secure it or gloriously die!

The Labourer toils and strives for more
While tyrants are carousing
But hark! I hear the lion roar
The British youths are rousing

The rich are liable to pain
The poor man feels the smart sir
But let us break the despot's chain
We soon will have the charter

Chorus
The Westgate Hotel straight to hell
We marched for our grievance was true sir
Down Stow hill for Redcoats to kill
But our reasons to fight were the truer

Cut down like corn on that winter morn
The boys of the Valleys forsaken
All came to nought though brave we fought
But our cause was never mistaken

Chorus

Written and arranged by Dawson Smith (Copyright 2005 C&P)

MY CHARTISTS' MARCH PILGRIMAGE

I parked my car near St Woolos Cathedral, a building of considerable antiquity. The name Woolos is a corruption of Gwynllyw, a Celtic prince who traditionally founded a mud and wattle oratory here in the early 6th century. The present church consists of a twelfth century Norman building enclosed within a later Medieval structure.

Opposite the *Six Bells Inn,* I ascended a short flight of steps to reach the high footway beside the cathedral and I looked up at the front of the impressive tower to pick out the disfigured effigy high up in its niche. It possibly represents Jasper Tudor who was responsible for the construction of the tower in the 14th century. The fact that it is one legged, armless and headless is explained by the tradition that it was used as target practice when Oliver Cromwell's men were in town.

I then looked across the roof tops on my right, towards Newport Docks and the steel girder Transporter Bridge straddling the river Usk, while in the distance the Bristol Channel gleamed in the morning sunlight.

As I descended Stow Hill I tried to imagine the marching Chartists flooding down the hill ahead of me. Wet and weary after their long journey, from places such as Nantyglo and Tredegar, many of the men by this time must have wondered what on earth they were doing here. Most of them were forced recruits anyway. But it must have been an incredible sight with 5,000 men marching down this hill into Newport which at that time had a population of just twelve thousand.

I passed Cross House on the corner of Havelock Street; identified by a small stone plaque on the wall. It is now the Baneswell Social Club and it is of interest that the Chartists' password on the day of the march was BEANS. The person who was challenged would then respond with the word WELL. Quite naturally it has become accepted that the word BEANSWELL was associated with the place Baneswell but it may be nothing more than coincidence. The original Welsh name probably meant 'The Stone Well' and this was later changed to Baneswell. The well was a natural spring beneath a rock at the foot of Stow Hill near Payne's Gate, which was the old name for the west gate of the town.

Cross House is named after a wayside preaching cross which used to stand at this spot and the base of it would still have been there when the Chartists marched past. It is reputed that Baldwin, Archbishop of Canterbury preached the Third Crusade here in 1188. The cross must have stood here for centuries before it was pulled down by Cromwell's men in the seventeenth century.

The Tower of St Woolos Church with its defaced effigy of Jasper Tudor

Remarkably, the head of the cross was discovered in 1926 by engineers constructing a new bridge across the Usk in Newport. It was buried deep in the mud about 40 yards from the town bank. By all accounts, Cromwell's Ironsides, having decapitated Jasper Tudor's effigy on St Woolos's tower, then knocked off the head of the cross and threw it into the River Usk.

At the bottom of Stow Hill I reached the old *Westgate Hotel* which stands on the site of an earlier building, made famous by the Chartist uprising. The name 'Westgate' dates back to the even earlier 'Westgate House' which stood on the same site in the 15th century. It belonged to Sir William ap Thomas, who resided at Raglan Castle and due to the colour of his armour was known as the 'Blue Knight'. When his daughter married Sir Henry Stradling of St Donat's Castle in Glamorgan, Westgate House formed part of her dowry. It was later sold to William Kemeys of Cefn Mably who became Constable of Newport Castle. Roger Kemeys, the last of the family sold it to Henry Morgan of Penllwyn Sarph in 1611. The house was rebuilt in 1779 and it then became known as the *Westgate Inn*.

Pigot and Co.'s Monmouthshire Directory 1822, gives the proprietors of the *Westgate Hotel* as being Messrs W. and S. Iggulden, who were there until 1838, when the business was taken over by Mr Samuel J. Hallen. He remained the proprietor for about the next 46 years.

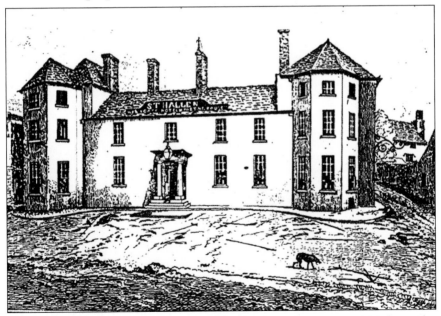

The *Westgate Hotel* was situated on one side of an irregular square, which forms the hub of the town centre where five important thoroughfares converge

Re-enactment by school children to mark the 150th anniversary
of the Chartists' uprising in 1989

Re-enactment of the scene outside the *Westgate Hotel* in 1839

The leading group of Chartists, led by John Rees, a stonemason from Tredegar, reached the Westgate Hotel at 9.20 a.m. They first tried to enter through the stable yard, but found that the gates were locked, so they went around to the square in front of the building. Here they found Thomas Bevan Oliver, a special constable and John o' Dwyer, a reporter from the *Monmouthshire Merlin*. The Mayor, Sir Thomas Phillips was standing bravely in the doorway. They had only expected to find a magistrate here, but Sir Thomas Phillips was an intelligent man and well informed of the Chartists' plans. He had quietly been making his own preparations in view of the reports that he had receieved the previous day.

Information obtained by spies and scouts had confirmed that the Chartists would be marching on Newport. Seventy Redcoats quartered in the workhouse, at the top of stow Hill, were alerted for action and Mayor Thomas Phillips summoned all the town's special constables to stand by as well.

When day dawned on Monday 4th November, reports were received that the marchers were approaching. The Mayor then sent a request to the barracks for military assistance. At this time there was only one company of soldiers stationed at Newport and these were of Her Majesty's 45th Regiment of foot. Thirty men under the command of Lieutenant Basil Gray were sent to give the Mayor assistance and they arrived at the Westgate Hotel at about 8.00 a.m. Prisoners who had been detained during the night, were placed in the cellars and soldiers were stationed in a room on the ground floor of the hotel.

The Mayor read the Riot Act, after which Superintendant Hopkins stood at the main entrance to the hotel with Constables Scard and Chappel, who had served with him in the Bristol Police Force. Just inside the door were special constables T. B. Oliver, a printer; John o'Dwyer, a reporter; Hopkins and Isaac Venn, bread and biscuit baker. Inside the hotel were special constables: Edmund Williams, Davies, licensee of the *Sailor's Return*, Joseph Adye, watchman; Richard Waters, attorney at law; Thomas Latch, William Jenkins, grocer and clerk of St Woolos Church; James Jones, tiler and plasterer; David Nedeck, clerk to David Williams, solicitor; William Henry Williams, accountant; Benjamin Gould, painter and glazier; M. Camden, master painter and Francis Kynvin, painter, plumber and glazier.

At 9.30 am a large body of Chartists arrived at the foot of Stow Hill, led by a man named Walters and they wheeled round to the right. Walters and some others made for the front door of the hotel, while others proceeded to the courtyard.

Sir Thomas Phillips bravely asked the mass of men before him to state their demands and in return Walters shouted, "Give us up the prisoners!" A special constable in the doorway shouted, "No never!"

Engraving, depicting the Chartists' attack on the *Westgate Hotel* in 1839

Walters forty years later described the attack as follows:

"I was one of the young fellows that used the hatchets against the big door of the Westgate Hotel, on November 3rd, 1839. We broke through and reached the passage beyond. The Redcoats were firing through the passage at the wild throng in the road, and we were in the midst of fire, smoke and awful cries. How I and the daring ones escaped I do not know. In the fight in the passage I happened to look down and saw my hand covered in blood and my finger gone. It had been carried away by one of the bullets of the soldiers when I was using the hatchet."

How the firing actually started is not certain, but it would seem that a Chartist opened fire first at one of the Special Constables and inspired the mob into action. Other men then fired and wounded several soldiers. At this point Mayor Phillips received a shot in the hip and his right arm and in the confusion a soldier was about to shoot him when someone shouted, "For God's sake, don't shoot the Mayor.". The front door of the inn was then slammed shut and the Chartists pounded on it, but their confidence quickly vanished when, on an order from the Mayor, the Redcoats opened fire.

After four volleys from the windows and down the passage towards the front door the mob was quickly dispersed. Within minutes, twenty two men lay dead or dying and fifty were wounded.

These wet and weary men who had little heart for a fight after their long march, fled in all directions, throwing their weapons on the ground and leaving their wounded companions, groaning, moaning and dying. It was all over in twenty five minutes.

In my imagination I saw the prostrate Chartists wounded, bleeding and dying outside the *Westgate Hotel* and thought of Alexander Cordell's description of the situation, as seen through the eyes of Iestyn Mortymer:

> *"Caught in the open by trained men under cover, the Chartists were breaking. The square was emptying, littered with writhing men, and arms; groans and cries rose from the smoke."*

> *"Under the portico of the mayor's house at the bottom of Stow Hill a man was dying - Abraham Thomas... And he called for the Charter now, his voice vibrant. .. Behind us the Chartists were dead or wounded, before us they lay under the scorching fire of the Redcoats. Only one fired back now, a man with one leg, the last broken hero of the Chartist cause."*

Dragging my mind back to the present, I followed shoppers along the pedestrianised street and made my way, past the bronze ox with a large bell on its back, to reach the colourful mural which dramatically illustrates the story of the Chartists' march and their skirmish outside the *Westgate Hotel*. Unfortunately, it is situated in a dark passageway, which makes it difficult to photograph unless one uses a flashgun. Two women carrying loaded shopping bags passed by and noticed me taking a picture. They both stopped and turned to look at the wall, curious to see what had caught my attention. One of them remarked in obvious surprise, "Well I never - I haven't noticed that 'muriel' before."

After taking my pictures I continued past some buskers who were using the passageway as an echo chamber to amplify their performance, and entered John Frost Square. It was packed with people, shoppers and relaxed senior citizens sitting around on the benches, enjoying the warm sunshine.

I made my way across the Square to Newport Museum and Library. Just inside the entrance, I paused in the museum shop to look at some of the books on sale, being particularly interested in those that dealt with the Chartists' uprising.

Mosaic, depicting the Chartists' march, John Frost Square, Newport

Mosaic, depicting the Chartists' attack on the *Westgate Hotel*, Newport

The main reason for my visit to the museum was to look at the section relating to the Chartists' march on Newport and shortly I found the panels that I had come to see. From the displayed newspaper cuttings I learned that fourteen Chartists were charged with High Treason at a special Assizes at Shire Hall on 31 December 1839. John Frost, Zephaniah Williams and William Jones the three leaders, were sentenced to be hanged and quartered. They spent three weeks in the condemned cell in Monmouth Gaol awaiting this sentence to be carried out. But fortunately for them, a nationwide campaign on their behalf resulted in their sentences being changed to transportation for life. In due course they were taken to a penal settlement in Tasmania and fifteen years later, in 1854, they were all given conditional pardons.

Also on display is a bust of John Frost, several pikes, pistols, homemade swords and an interesting piece of protective headgear in the form of an iron cap covered with cloth. In addition there is a policeman's truncheon of the period and several Chartist handbills.

One exhibition case features Sir Thomas Phillips, Mayor of Newport at the time of the uprising. During the attack on the Westgate he was wounded in the arm and hip, and generally regarded as the hero of the hour. In due course he was given the freedom of the city of London and he even dined with Queen Victoria at Windsor Castle, where he received a knighthood.

On his return to Newport he was presented with a silver service valued at 800 guineas. It comprised a candelabra, one soup toureen, one venison dish, four other dishes, a silver plate, two vases and four entree dishes with covers.

Of particular interest is an audio tape which one listens to through a telephone handpiece. The narration and sound effects tell the story of the Chartists' march on Newport and it is most realistic and informative.

I left the museum and made my way back through the town to the *Westgate Hotel* where an inuagural banquet took place on 5th May 1886, to celebrate its reconstruction. The *Monmouthshire Merlin* records that:

> " *The well known hostelry the Westgate was kept for many years by the late Mr. Hallen. The old building will be remembered by everyone who has seen Newport, and the old pillars which were perforated by Chartist bullets are the only things now left of the old pile. These have been utilized by the architect of the present building in the vestibule of the hotel, where they are doing duty as supports to the ornamental moulding. The bullet holes still remain, and the old pillars are preserved intact.*"

When these pillars were removed on 17th September 1884 during the reconstruction of the building, the hollow pillars were found to contain four roughly made bullets or slugs which had evidently lain there since the day of the attack - forty five years before.

My mind then returned to the day when bodies lay scattered around the Westgate Square. Some of the wounded men had managed to escape but others managed to get away for only a short distance. One man named Lovell, who carried a gun and was wounded in the thigh got no further than the corner of Skinner Street and he lay there in agony for some time pleading for assistance. Eventually he was carried away and taken to the home of a Mr. Jenkins, where he was put to bed and his wound given attention.

Another Chartist who had received a gunshot wound, had managed to crawl on his hands and knees across the road where he collapsed under the portico of the Mayor's house at the bottom of Stow Hill. As he lay dying, he apparently shouted, "The Charter for ever!"

Bodies lay scattered around the outside of the *Westgate Hotel* all that day until it was eventually decided that they should be taken away. They were removed on stretchers and laid out in the hotel stables to await an inquest.

The following bodies were identified:-

William Williams of Cwmtillery, George Shell of Pontypool,
Abraham Thomas of Coalbrookvale, William Evans of Tredegar,
Isaac Thomas of Nantyglo, William Griffiths of Merthyr and
William Farraday of Blackwood.

Section from the mural near John Frost Square, Newport

A young woman who forced her way through the crowd of spectators into the stable yard and saw the dead bodies lying there, immediately threw herself upon one of them with a loud scream. It was her husband and she was gently dragged away from him smeared with his blood. Only ten bodies were actually laid out in the stable yard at the *Westgate Hotel* but the *Monmouthshire Merlin* reported twenty two deaths which was probably the true figure.

In 1989, some modern sculptures, commissioned by Newport Borough Council and designed by Christopher Kelly, were erected outside the old *Westgate Hotel* to commemorate the 150th anniversary of the Chartists' uprising and the tragic events which took place here in 1839. The three groups take their title from the motto of the Chartist convention: 'Union, Prudence, Energy'.

These bronze sculptures outside the old *Westgate Hotel* were commissioned by Newport Borough Council as a permanent reminder of the Chartist Movement. They were unveiled on the 4th November 1989 on the 150th anniversary of the dramatic events which took place in this square.

The figures representing 'Union' carry a model of Newport surrounded by dancing children. 'Prudence' is depicted by two figures representing the arts, commerce and industry which have played an important part in the fortunes of Newport, past and present. 'Energy' consists of three recumbent figures which lie seemingly crushed, but representing the foundation from which the spirit of Chartism sprang.

John Frost was born in the *Royal Oak Inn*, Thomas Street (long demolished)

I next went in search of the birthplace of John Frost which would have been in Thomas Street opposite the *King's Head Hotel*. But the site is now occupied by a modern building called 'The Corn Exchange' and a sign informed me that it was the Newport City Council office for Social Wellbeing and Housing.

Some years earlier I had seen a plaque here commemorating the birth of John Frost who first saw light of day in the *Royal Oak* in 1786, a few yards away, but sadly the plaque has been removed.

It had been unveiled by the mayor of Newport, Alderman J.R. Wardell on Friday 3rd November 1939 at 11.30 a.m. on the eve of the centenary of the Chartist uprising. Two or three hundred people gathered in Thomas Street that day to watch the ceremony and this was the only public activity undertaken by the Chartist Centenary Celebrations Committee in view of the Second World War. Representatives of the town and county mingled with the crowd who watched the unveiling of this memorial to John Frost who, in the words of the mayor, "was a man of vision, but not always of sound judgement."

After the ceremony the guests walked across the road to the *King's Head Hotel*, where speeches were made and light refreshments served on the site of the room where John Frost was taken before being conveyed to Monmouth for trial.

The Murenger House in High Street was once the home of John Frost

Walking back down High Street I passed the Murenger House (c.1535), where John Frost resided for a short time. Apart from St Woolos Cathedral it is the oldest surviving building in Newport and it is believed to have once been the town house of Sir Charles Herbert of Troy, near Monmouth. He was Sheriff of the county in the 16th century. At a later date it was occupied by the Murenger who was an official responsible for the upkeep of the town walls and tolls were collected for this purpose. From that time it has always been known as the Murenger House. Above the entrance a colourful sign shows the Murenger inspecting work being done to the town walls.

Returning to the *Westgate Hotel*, I walked back up Stow Hill and began thinking of the tail enders of the 5,000 men who must have fled from the horrific scene outside the old inn. Many of them of course never reached the Westgate Square and no doubt hurried straight back up the hill when they heard the muskets firing. According to the *Monmouthshire Merlin*:-

> *"The heat of the conflict lasted about a quarter of an hour, when the defeated Chartists took to their heels in all directions - throwing away their arms and abandoning their dead and dying and we are credibly informed that the Chartists who were at the rear of the column up Stow Hill, fled across fields below the church, in all directions scattering their weapons as they went, and appearing panic-stricken on hearing the roll of musketry. "*

One hundred and fifty weapons of varying types thrown down by the fleeing Chartists outside the *Westgate Hotel* were subsequently collected together and taken to Cross House on Stow Hill which, then was the residence of Mr. Hopkins the Superintendant of the Borough Police Force. There were guns, pistols, blunderbusses, swords, bayonets, daggers, pikes, spears, billhooks, reaping hooks, hatchets, cleavers, axes, pitchforks, blades of knifes, scythes and saws fitted in staves; rods of iron, two or three yards in length, sharpened at one end; bludgeons of various length and size; hand and sledge hammers and mandrills.

At the top of Stow Hill I walked through the churchyard and reached the north side where ten of the dead Chartists were buried in three graves. Unfortunately, a road has been cut through that area and their graves (unmarked) were probably destroyed.

But standing there I looked down on the town and saw the modern office block named the Chartist Tower directly opposite, and I thought of its significance. It bears the name of the Chartists and can thus be regarded as a twentieth century monument to the men who died on that fateful day in 1839.

In 1988 Alexander Cordell unveiled a memorial plaque near the entrance to St Woolos Cathedral to commemorate the Chartists who were buried nearby in 1839.

It reads:

> 'This plaque commemorating the Chartists killed in the battle outside the Westgate Hotel was set into the bank near the lychgate of St Woolos Church in 1988 and was financed by Newport Local History Society and Newport Borough Council. It was unveiled by Alexander Cordell.'

Memorial to the fallen Chartists, St Woolos Cathedral

On 18th April 1840 the *Monmouthshire Merlin* reported that the Chartist graves had been decked with flowers and laurels surmounted with the following verse:

> 'May the rose of England never blow,
> The Clyde of Scotland cease to flow,
> The harp of Ireland never play,
> Until the Chartists gain the day. '

For many years red roses were left on the burial place of these men on the anniversary of their death. This custom was revived in 1985 by members of Newport Local History Society, who wished to keep alive the memory of those who fought and died in Newport for principles and rights, which are today largely taken for granted. It is perhaps more than coincidence that the Labour Party adopted the red rose as their new symbol in 1987.

Inside the cathedral I found two interesting wall tablets which commemorate two people associated with the industrial history of old Monmouthshire. The first one informed me that the mortal remains of the Reverend Matthew Monkhouse, formerly of Sirhowy Ironworks, magistrate and Deputy Lieutenant for the County of Monmouth, are deposited in a vault beneath the organ. He died on December 5th 1822 aged 62 years.

The other tablet of significance is on the wall of the Crindau Chapel and it commemorates Benjamin Pratt who was once a director of the Blaenafon Ironworks. This Worcestershire man was born in 1742 and he came to the Pontypool area in 1785 to become a partner of Thomas Hill and Thomas Hopkins who established the Blaenafon Ironworks in 1789.

Pratt died suddenly at the *Angel Hotel* in Abergavenny, whilst stopping for a meal with a friend, on his way to Blaenafon. He rose from his chair to ring for the waiter and suddenly felt giddy. Sitting down, he exclaimed "I am going to die, - but I die an honest man!" and promptly expired.

As I stood reading Benjamin Pratt's memorial tablet, one of the chaplains came up and spoke to me. We chatted for a while about the fascinating history of St Woolos Cathedral and I told him of my interest in the Chartists who were buried nearby. He then invited me to inspect the register in the Vestry and showed me the entry concerning these men.

"Buried at once in (?) graves. Ten men unknown, shot by a party of the 45th Reg. of Foot in a Chartist Insurrection before the Westgate Inn Nov 4th 1839. Abode not known. Buried on November 7th."

Among the dead was George Shell, a lad of nineteen, who was shot down in the passage of the *Westgate Hotel* entrance by one of the soldiers. The night before, young George had sent a brief note to his parents:-

Pontypool
Sunday Night
November 3, 1839.

Dear Parents, - I hope this will find you well, as I am myself at this present. I shall this night be engaged in a glorious struggle for freedom and should it please God to spare my life I shall see you soon; but if not, grieve not for me - I shall have fallen in a noble cause. Farewell.

Yours truly,
George Shell

Capture of the Ringleaders

Bills were immediately posted, offering rewards of £100 each for the capture of John Frost, Zephaniah Williams and William Jones. Frost had been seen soon after the Westgate fiasco, walking briskly through Tredegar Park, holding a handkerchief to his face, as if he was crying. He then took to the woods in the direction of Cardiff, and near Castleton, he hid himself in a coal tram. There he stayed for eight hours and when dusk came, walked stealthily back to Newport. He entered the house of Partridge the printer who had worked closely with him, producing a range of material to promote the Chartist cause. His printed material which can be seen in Newport Museum includes a letter to the Working Men of Monmouthshire and the address and rules of the Workingman's Association, which was the political body of the Chartists.

Frost was made welcome and hidden between some mattresses. The police knocked on the door and Partridge opened it and said, "We are all in bed." However, the police forced their way in, arrested Frost and Partridge, and took them to the *Westgate Hotel*.

William Jones was captured a few weeks later in a wood near the Navigation Inn, Crumlin. He threatened his pursuers with a pistol, but then gave himself up.

Zephaniah Williams managed to evade capture for three weeks, having reached his home to obtain money. He then made for Cardiff and boarded a merchant ship called *Vantage*. The Cardiff police came on board the ship at three o'clock in the morning of 23rd November, on the day it was due to sail for Portugal. They woke up a man who gave his name as Thomas Jones of Bridgend, but eventually admitted that he was Zephaniah Williams. He was immediately taken to Newport and kept handcuffed to an officer night and day until he arrived in Monmouth Gaol.

NEWPORT RIOTS
£300 Reward

ZEPHANIAH WILLIAMS, a native of Argoed, Bedwellty, in the County of Monmouth, coal agent, and who lately kept the *King Crispin* beerhouse at Blaina: about 5' 8" high, strong square built, dark hair, no whiskers, round smooth face, full dark hazel eyes, very short necked, nose inclined to turn a little, pale complexion, rather blunt manner and bold talker; has the appearance of a seafaring man and loose swagger; usually wore a black coat and dark trousers; a small neck handkerchief round his neck showing a shirt collar.

My Journey Home

Just outside Newport, I turned off the A4042 and drove through the sprawl of Bettws housing estate in search of the little church from which Bettws takes its name. It was in this ancient church, dedicated to St. David that John Frost (at the age of 28 years) married Mary Geach, a Newport Widower, on 24th October 1812. John Frost was a Nonconformist and a member first of Mill Street Congregational Church and then a church in Dock Street which in later years was converted into Newport's Little Theatre.

Inside Bettws Church are some stained glass windows which commemorate Thomas Protheroe, who lived at Malpas Court and contributed £250 towards the re-building of this church in 1858. He was an arch enemy of John Frost and became a wealthy man by unscrupulous and devious means.

St David's Church Bettws

Driving on to Llantarnam, I stopped briefly at an interesting old coaching inn called *The Greenhouse*. Above the porch is a sign bearing a Welsh inscription which has been translated as reading:-

The Green House
1719
Good Beer
And Cider for you
Come in
You shall taste it.

The *Greenhouse Inn*, Llantarnam

The *Upper Cock Inn*, Croesyceiliog, sketched by Fred Hando in 1923

Outside this inn, on the morning of November 4 1839, the Chartists from the Eastern Valley were confronted by Mr. R. J. Blewitt, M.P. for Monmouth Borough, who lived at Llantarnam Abbey. They listened to his words of warning with respect, but still continued with their march via Malpas and Barrack Hill to the rendezvous point at Cefn.

I drove on, inhaling the sickly smell of warm biscuits coming from Burton's Biscuit Factory and thought what it must have been like to have been a hungry Chartist marching to Newport in 1839. A mile later, I made a detour to take in the village of Croesyceiliog.

Here the Eastern Valley marchers, led by William Jones had halted at the *Upper Cock Inn* at about 1.00 a.m. They took refreshment and nonchantly dried their damp gunpowder in an oven!

I recalled how the Gwent historian Fred Hando described the time in 1923, when he visited this inn and met "a bright eyed lady of Croesyceiliog." She told him that she had been born in the *Upper Cock* in July 1839..."So I don't remember much about the visit of the Chartists. My parents often told me how the men charged into the inn demanding drinks, and calling on all the men to join them. You should really see Mrs. Lewis, widow of John Lewis the runner."

Fred then went in search of Mrs. Lewis and found her in a low one-storeyed thatched cottage near the foot of the hill. "Her husband - a remarkable athlete worked at Llanyrafon Mill and at 69 had won a 100 yards race at Cwmbran."

Old Mrs. Lewis told Fred that "when the Chartists called at this cottage John Lewis three days old was lying in the arms of his mother. They entered and searched every room. In the bedroom the mother held the baby towards them saying, 'Here's the only man in the house; take him with pleasure' - and all the time her husband was hiding under the yew tree in the opposite field."

From Croesyceiliog I drove on to Llanelen and parked my car near the village hall. This is a quiet liitle village which at one time boasted three inns, *The Hanbury*, *The lion* and the *Butchers' Arms*. But today the village is 'dry,' for in the 19th century, Lady Llanover, who was strongly opposed to her tenants drinking, closed two of the inns down and converted the other into a temperance house.

Opposite the village hall I walked up St Helen's Close and made my way to the church which is dedicated to St Elen, a daughter of Prince Eudaf of Ewyas. According to Welsh tradition she married Magnus Clemens Maximus, who became Emperor in Britain, Gaul and Spain from AD 383 - 388.

On arriving at the church, I remembered that Thomas Phillips the heroic Mayor of Newport used to live in this village and was buried here. My first thought was that there would surely be a memorial tablet to this local celebrity inside the church, so I sought the key at a house on the other side of the churchyard, and within a few minutes I was standing inside the church. But I looked in vain and quickly realised that Llanelen had not honoured its famous inhabitant in this way.

After returning the key, I began scouring the churchyard, reading all the inscriptions. Eventually I came to the top corner and peered over some iron railings and found the last resting place of Thomas Phillips and also his parents. The inscription reads as follows:-

'Sacred to the memory of Thomas Phillips,
born in Llantilio Pertholey 18th December
1745. Also of Ann his wife, born at
Crickhowell 7th July 1775; died in
this parish 6 October 1854.

Also in memory of their eldest son
Sir Thomas Phillips Knt., Queen's
Council, Bencher of the Inner Temple;
born 16th September 1801, died 26th
May 1867.'

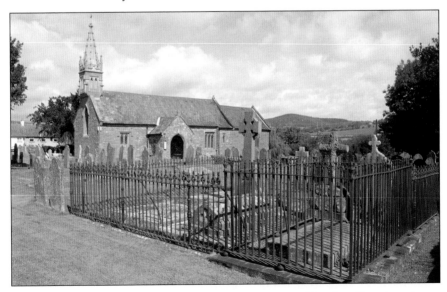

The grave of Sir Thomas Phillips and his parents in Llanelen Churchyard

Thomas Phillip's father (also named Thomas) was of humble birth and worked as a cinder-tip labourer at the Ebbw Vale Ironworks, but his wife Ann is said to have descended from Sir Dafydd Gam, a hero of the battle of Agincourt in 1415. This brave man was knighted whilst he lay dying on the battlefield having just helped to save the life of King Henry V.

So perhaps it is fitting that the son of Davy Gam's descendant, Mayor Phillips, was knighted for his bravery after the *Westgate* affair. He received his knighthood and dined with Queen Victoria at Windsor Castle in December 1839.

In his memoirs Lord Grenville remembered the occasion as follows:-

"On Monday last, I went to Windsor for a council. There we had Sir Thomas Phillips, Mayor of Newport, who came to be knighted. They were going to knight him and dismiss him; but I persuaded Normanby that it would be a wise and popular thing to keep him there. Normanby said that etiquette did not permit one of Phillips's rank in life to be invited to the royal table. I said this was all nonsense; if he was good enough to be knighted, he was good enough to dine there. He was convinced, spoke to Melbourne, who settled it, and Phillips stayed. Nothing could have answered better; everybody approved of it, and the man behaved as if his whole life had been spent in courts, perfectly at ease, without rudeness or forwardness, quiet, unobtrusive, but with complete self-possession and a nil admirari manner which had something distinguished in it. The Queen was very civil to him and he was delighted."

At the age of 18, Phillips was articled to Thomas Prothero, a Newport solicitor, Town Clerk of Newport and agent of Sir Charles Morgan. Thomas Phillips himself later became Town Clerk of Newport and was made Mayor in 1838.

In 1842, Sir Thomas Phillips was called to the Bar at the Inner Temple and a few years later was one of the founders of Trinity College Carmarthen. He built a school in Llanelen for 81 pupils in 1848 and during that year was made Deputy Lieutenant for the County of Monmouth, Governor of King's College London and Chairman of the Society of Arts.

He bought Llanelen House which adjoins the churchyard in about 1840. However, during the greater part of his life he lived in London and used Llanelen as an occasional country residence.

Although he is best known for the part he played as Mayor of Newport in the Westgate, it should be remembered that Sir Thomas Phillips was also a scholar who wrote several books, including one published in 1849 entitled, *Wales, the Language and Social Conditions* and in 1850 he wrote a biography entitled *The Life of James Davies, a Schoolmaster*.

Sir Thomas Phillips died in London on Sunday 26th May 1867. The previous Tuesday he had been addressing a committe of the House of Commons, when, resuming his seat, he was struck with a paralysis.

At his request he was buried in Llanelen churchyard in the most simple fashion, from his residence, Llanelen House. The ceremony was conducted by the Bishop of Llandaff, the Rev W. Jones Llanellen, the Rev Rees Jones Penmaen and the Rev Canon W. Price.

Just below Llanelen Church is the Old Vicarage which Alexander Cordell was renting when he began writing *Rape of the Fair Country*. But the strange thing for me is that he nearly wrote the book in my cottage at Llanfoist. I remember we had just returned there after a research trip in the Clydach Gorge and Alex, with his mug of coffee, half-way to his lips, suddenly said, "It is strange sitting here, for this cottage came on the market when I was writing *Rape of the Fair Country*. The owner was asking £1,000 and I couldn't afford it. But if I had bought it, then *Rape of the Fair Country* would have been written here!"

The *Old Vicarage* in Llanelen is where Alexander Cordell lived, when he began writing his most famous novel *Rape of the Fair Country*

Stone bridge spanning the river Usk at Llanelen

Today, the stone bridge spanning the Usk at Llanelen is busy with traffic and if crossing it on foot one has to take great care. When Cordell lived in Llanelen in the 1950s the traffic would have been much more infrequent. He no doubt walked down here and standing on the bridge imagined Iestyn Mortymer relating how he had been lying on the bank of the Usk *'with the music of the river flowing over me. Weeds waved, stones shimmered, insects droned. This was the way to fish - with the fingers.'* It was then that Iestyn spotted his future wife, Mari Dirion, bathing naked in the river:

> *'There is a salmon for you - five feet long if he is an inch, and well over a hundred pounds - a hen salmon, by the look of it - standing on its tail in three feet of water, throwing its white arms about and combing out its long, black hair.'*

I remember Alex once telling me that before he wrote *Rape of the Fair Country*, he had been an admirer of the novels of Richard Vaughan, who wrote about a farming community based around the little village of Llanddeusant in Carmarthenshire. The name Dirion was in fact borrowed from Richard Vaughan's book *Moulded in Earth*.

PAN GIANT

THE HOSTS OF REBECCA
Alexander Cordell

THE TREMENDOUS
SUCCESSOR TO
RAPE OF THE
FAIR COUNTRY

Running over with lust
and strength ... sin and
righteousness THE TIMES

3/6

THE HOSTS OF REBECCA

In November 1959, Alexander Cordell commented that he had received hundreds of letters from readers of *Rape of the Fair Country* asking him to write the continuing story of the Mortymer family. He confirmed that this was indeed his intention:

> "I am now doing this in a new novel which is set in Carmarthenshire with the Rebecca riots as a background. My working title is *Cry of a Fair People* but it may well be something different when it is published. It was my original intention to tell the twin story of Chartism and Rebeccaism in one book but so much material came to light during research that it was impossible within the confines of one novel. This new book will deal with the years 1839-43, the period immediately following that in which *Rape of the Fair Country* was set."

In due course this book was published under the title *The Hosts of Rebecca*. Cordell was employed at this time as a Quantity Surveyor based in Abergavenny and he had to visit the area where *The Hosts of Rebecca* is placed during the course his work. This was fortunate, for it enabled him to carry out research at the same time.

REVIEWS OF *THE HOSTS OF REBECCA*

"Mr Cordell has more than fulfilled the promise of his first book *Rape of the Fair Country* "

News Chronicle

"The second book is the big test of the novelist's stamina. Here is Mr Cordell taking it in his stride. *The Hosts of Rebecca* has the attack and pristine zest which you associate with a 'debut'. It is on the boil non-stop, a singular combination of action and emotion"

Maurice Richardson *Observer*

"Page after page of this racy and vivid story can be read as easily as though it were listened to in some snug bar parlour. Another best-seller."

Rosaleen Whately, *Liverpool Post*

The Hosts of Rebecca was published in the USA under the title *The Robe of Honour.*

"As he chronicled in *The Rape of the Fair Country* the savage Chartist riots in Monmouthshire, so in *The Robe of Honour* Cordell chronicles the equally savage Rebecca riots in Carmarthenshire. The first riots centered on the iron mines; the Rebeccas fought in coal country, though their movement originally was an agricultural protest.

Garbed in Klondike petticoats, they warred on the tollgates erected by absentee landlords to exact tribute from them on every road they travelled to market with their products so that, in the end, their profits were eaten up before they reached the market. As with the Chartists, the Rebeccas were beaten into bloody submission but, ultimately, in both cases, the uprising brought reforms.

Cordell writes with wondrous compassion of the pitiful condition of the poor as the whole teeming countryside brawls and riots in open rebellion. The book is rich in the sights and sounds of the countryside. It is with *Rape of the Fair Country*, a novel to take to your heart.

Chicago *Sunday Tribune*

"Taken together, *The Rape of the Fair Country* and T*he Robe of Honour* are superb. Mr Cordell spares nothing in portraying the indescribable lot of the masses under absentee landlords and yet his book is shot through with wonderfully robust humour and with descriptions of the countryside that clutch at the throat.

This novel is intense, vivid, violent fiction mirroring a time and a place in a manner reminiscent of Dylan Thomas."

Omaha *World Herald*

JOURNEY TO CARMARTHENSHIRE

*"The door of the coach slammed shut, a whip cracked, and the hooves
of the horses clattered. Mari called again, her voice breaking. I waited
in the teeming rain and saw the coach up Turnpike. I stayed until it
was outlined against the sky over Garndyrus; saw it slowly
disappear over the crest to Abergavenny."*

These were Iestyn's words describing the departure of the surviving
members of the Mortymer family from Blaenavon. He had chosen to stay
behind, having made the decision to fight for the Charter and join the
march on Newport.

Standing outside the *Cordell Country Inn*, I imagined the coach carrying
Mam Mortymer, Morfydd, Mari and the children Richard and Jonothan
descend the hill towards Abergavenny on their way to a new life in
Carmarthenshire.

With these thoughts in my mind, I followed in their wake, driving down
the side of the Blorenge Mountain and through Govilon to pick up the A40
at Crickhowell. Then on over the Bwlch Pass and past the so familiar, but
always impressive skyline of the Brecon Beacons; to take the 20th century
Brecon by-pass; then on through Sennybridge, Trecastle, Llandovery,
Llandeilo, and through the beautiful Vale of Towi, to reach Abergwili on
the outskirts of Carmarthen where I had planned my first stop.

Carmarthen Museum at Abergwili

Originally founded in 1908 by the Carmarthenshire Antiquarian Society
Carmarthen Museum is now housed in the former palace of the Bishop of
St David's, which dates back to the 13th century. Inside the museum is a
wide range of information and displays relating to Carmarthen and the
local area.

My main reason for coming to this museum was to seek information on
the Rebecca riots and I found that this historic event is briefly mentioned in
a room upstairs. There is a display case containing a part-time constable's
baton which was apparently used during the Rebecca Riots in Carmarthen
in 1845. In addition there is a pair of flintlock pistols, dating to the same
period.

An oil painting depicts Captain David Davies of Trawsmawr, who in
1843 played a part in dealing with the Rebecca riots in Carmarthen.
Nearby, is a panel briefly outlining the story of 'Rebecca and her
Daughters' and the riots that took place in Carmarthenshire from 1839-
1844.

Carmarthen Museum is housed in the old Bishop's Palace at Abergwili

A fine example of a toll house in the grounds of Carmarthen Museum

On my return to the car park I noticed a Toll house, in good condition, but obviously unused, near the entrance to the museum, and at one time beside the main road. Here, to my mind would be a golden opportunity for the museum to set up an additional point of historical interest. The interior could be used to house a display on the history of Toll Gates and the story of the Rebecca Riots. Perhaps the curator of Carmarthen Museum will one day read these comments and take action.

Carmarthen

I pressed on into Carmarthen and after finding a convenient car park, I took a stroll around the town. It certainly has a long history, for in ancient times the Goidelic tribe of Demetae had their headquarters in a hill-fort which they built on a rise facing the river.

When the Romans arrived here in 74 -77 they built a garrison fort, which they called Moridinum, from the Celtic *mor* meaning sea, and *dunum*, the Celtic word for fortress. This was the Romans' most westerly defensive position in Britain.

The old Welsh name for the town is Caerfyrddin and the 12th century chronicler Geoffrey of Monmouth mistakenly linked the name with Myrddin - the Welsh version of Merlin - thus establishing the tradition that it was "Merlin's Town." A stump of an old oak tree known as "Merlin's Oak" used to stand at the junction of Priory Street and Oak Lane. Local folklore and tradition attributed to Merlin the prophecy that "when Merlin's Oak tree shall tumble down, then shall fall Carmarthen town."

However, the tree is said to have sprung from an acorn planted by a local schoolmaster on 19th May 1659, to mark the accession of Charles II. At the beginning of the 19th century it was poisoned by a local tradesman who became fed up with the local people gathering there for meetings.

In December 1901 the Borough Council decided that steps should be taken to preserve a young tree growing beside the old oak and that "an iron guard be placed around the young tree by the Old Oak in Priory Street and such means as are possible be taken to preserve the old oak." However, the old oak in fact outlasted the sapling. The final remains of Merlin's oak were removed by the Council and taken to St Peter's Civic Hall in 1978, and put on display. A fragment of the tree may also be seen in the museum at Abergwili.

In Nott Square I found the old gatehouse to Carmarthen Castle, which is virtually all that remains of this once proud fortress built to command the Town. It was originally erected on the orders of William Rufus in 1093 as a wooden structure on an earthen mound and later replaced with a stone

80

castle. This survived intact until the Civil War and in 1660 it was recorded as being "quite demolished."

Carmarthen Gaol was built in 1789 on the site of the castle by the architect John Nash (later to become famous as the builder of Buckingham Palace). It was demolished in 1938 to make way for the new County Hall which was completed in 1948.

The old gatehouse to Carmarthen Castle

Carmarthen Castle stands on the site of a hill-fort built by the Demetae tribe

The Guildhall in Carmarthen is where the trials of Shoni Sgubor Fawr (John Jones), Dai'r Cantwr (David Davies) and thirty-six other Rebecca rioters took place in December 1843.

Leaving Carmarthen, I crossed the rover Towy and followed the A484 south to Kidwelly, with the intention of searching for Cae White Farm where Cordell placed the Mortymer family.

Kidwelly (Cidweli)

Kidwelly is situated between the Gwendraeth Fach and the Gwendraeth Fawr which both feed into a wide inlet to the west of the town. It was once a larger port but unfortunately the harbour began to silt up in the 16th century and the town declined as a trading centre for about two hundred years. But the coal trade in the 19th century brought a revival in the town's fortunes and new quays were built and shipbuilding took place here.

It is a larger place than I expected and as a starting point, I made my way towards the impressive ruins of Kidwelly Castle which stands on a hill overlooking the Gwendraeth Fach. The first castle was built in 1114 by Roger, Bishop of Salisbury. He constructed a wooden tower two storeys high which was protected by a ditch and a wooden stockade.

French, Flemish and English settlers were brought here to live in the southern bailey of the castle and gradually the settlement grew into a town. At first it was known as Coetgueli which later became Cidweli and this was anglicised to Kidwelly.

In 1136 the local Welsh endeavoured to drive out the Normans and whilst her husband Gruffydd ap Rhys was in Gwynedd seeking reinforcements, Princess Gwenllian and her two young sons bravely marched on Kidwelly, at the head of a small but determined force. They fought the soldiers of Maurice de Londres, Lord of Kidwelly, in a field near the castle.

The battle was over in a very short time for Gwenllian's men were easily overwhelmed and the brave princess was severely wounded. Her young son Maelgwyn was killed by her side, while feebly endeavouring to shield his heroic mother from the blows of the enemy. Both Gwenllian and her other young son were captured and Lord Maurice immediately gave orders for the Welsh princess to be beheaded in his presence. The site where this sad event took place is on the eastern bank of the Gwendraeth Fach river and it is known as Maes Gwenllian (Field of Gwenllian).

In 1274 the wooden castle was replaced with a stone fortress which was started by Pain de Chaworth. Further developments took place in the 14th century under Henry of Lancaster, when an outer curtain wall, flanking towers, a chapel and a gatehouse were built.

The original town in the southern bailey had by this time been replaced by a new town, built on the other side of the river by the priory, and the old town was abandoned.

Kidwelly Castle stands on a hill overlooking the Gwendraeth Fach

In need of some refreshment I entered the *Boot & Shoe Inn*, just below the castle gatehouse, and sat down in the bar to study the Ordnance Survey map of the locality. Now, where could Cae White be placed? I knew from a conversation that I once had with Alex, on this very subject, that the building as such did not really exist. But that was not good enough for me for I wanted to give it a feasible location. So, consulting my well thumbed copy of the *The Hosts of Rebecca*, I drew up a list of useful clues.

(1) *It was a two mile walk along the river to Ponty....*

(2) *Cae White was stuck in the middle of Squire's acres as a ship in full sail.*

(3) *Beautiful was this old Welsh gentry place gone to ruin, standing in its thirty acres with pride of nobility, shunning lesser neighbours.*

Thus Cae White should be placed about two miles from Pontyberem and near the Gwendraeth Fawr. Also, it must be a solitary farmhouse surrounded by fields, but there would also have to be a chapel not far away, and a pub, for old Granfer was a regular visitor to the *Black Boar* tavern.

> *"The sheep track from Cae White leads to Black Boar Tavern, a track that carries the refuse of the north; the Midland drovers with their stinks, ghosts of the transportation hulks and prison, the fire-scarred puddlers of the Monmouthshire iron - not a pint of good Welsh blood in a thousand; all flocking to the coal industry of Carmarthenshire and to Betsi's place, the strongest ale in the country."*

> *"Strange that I knew Cae White was mine the moment I set foot in it; that I would shoulder the burden that Mari's grandfather had carried for life, and mate with it, and bring it to flower. Beautiful was this old Welsh gentry place gone to ruin, standing in its thirty acres with pride and nobility, shunning lesser neighbours."*

I came to realise that these clues could only provide an approximate location for Cae White, because Cordell used a variety of places that were not necessarily exaclty where he described them.

The best location that I could identify for Cae White Farm was Pen-y-maes, a farm situated just over a mile from a chapel at Bancycapel and about 2 miles north of Llandyfaelog, where the *Red Lion* could have served as Cordell's 'Black Boar Tavern', to which led a *"sheep track from Cae White"*.

> *" I remember with joy the early spring days in the new county, especially the Sundays in the pews of the Horeb. Mam one side of me, Morfydd on the other, she with an eye for every pair of trews in sight, until she caught my mother's glance which set her back miles. .....*
> *Little Meg Benyon was hitting it up on the harmonium, eyes on sticks, feet going, tongue peeping out between her white teeth, one missing; with Dai Altwen Preacher beating time and the tenors soaring and basses grovelling."*

A short distance west of Pen-y-maes is Parry's Castle which inspired the name for the character Squire Parry. Slightly further west is "Towy Castle", which is well suited for the fictitious home of Squire Parry. Now a residential home, it is a grand country house set in beautiful grounds overlooking the Towi, and ajoining Towy Castle Farm.

The *Red Lion* at Llandyfaelog

Bancycapel is conveniently sited

Towy Castle is where Cordell's Squire Parry could have lived

"Some nights, when we first came to Cae White, I would walk in the darkness to Squire's Reach and watch the comings and goings behind the lace-covered windows. There... I would see the gentry; the men, elegant in their frock coats, bowing to carpets; slim men, tall, the pick of the English officers, some billeted there to put down Rebecca."

Cordell, with his fascination for industry, decided that Jethro and Morfydd would seek employment in a local coal mine in order to bring in some much needed money. Early one morning they walk to Ponty (Pontyberem), which is much further than the 2 miles mentioned in the book, but certainly not too far away.

"The windows winked with light from the blackness as we took the road to coal... It was a 2 mile walk to Ponty and the mountain behind us frowned blue with the promise of dawn."

"The light of Gower's mine winked through the mist as we climbed the last hillock to Ponty. This, a green land ten years back, was now outraged. For the new indusry of coal was treading on the skirts of iron and the black diamond wealth of my country was making fortunes for men who had never set foot in Wales."

"Across the blackened tips went Morfydd and me to the ragtailed, heaving labourers staggering under their baskets of coal - women and children, mostly, cheaper labour than men. Little ones bent under loads, their stoops a perpetual; deformity that jack-knifed them over the eating tables and doubled them in their beds; black-faced, white-teethed; spewed from the womb of a deeper world, chanting to the labour of the stamping trot; a tuneless breath of a song that kept them to the rhythm, this, the night shift ending in exhaustion. Eyes peeped at the strangers, heads turned under baskets, but the labour never faltered, and the shale trembled to hobnail stamping. And we stood in the misted air, me and Morfydd, and watched the ants; watched them building the ant-hill high; chanting, scurrying, one eye open for Foreman - building up the monuments that future generations will despise, sweating and dying for their ninepence a day."

The shaft was descended by a series of ladders which were also the only means of bringing the coal out of the mine.

"A hundred feet down is a platform of light and the two ladders are snakes that reach to the bottom, baskets coming up one side, baskets going down on the other.

"You first," said Morfydd, and I saw the sweat suddenly bright on her face, for she had never done ladders before, and I wondered at her head for heights. Job Gower was behind us as I swung myself into space and gripped the rungs, and I saw the shadow of Morfydd's leg come over me as I went down hand over hand. Twenty feet down I stopped, for a woman was climbing against the platform of light, and her gasps were preceding her on the swaying rungs.

"Down with you," roared Job from the top. "Don't mind old Towey, plenty of room to pass."

Down, down, hand over hand, with the ladder bucking and the coal dust flying up, sucked upward by the draught. Looked up at the light above me and the morning clouds and saw Morfydd coming after me, her fingers peaked white on the rungs, skirts and petticoats

"A hundred feet down is a platform of light and the two ladders are snakes that reach to the bottom, baskets coming up one side, baskets going down the other."

billowing indecent, and I knew she was fearing the drop. Began to wonder how I could break her if she came, hang on and elbow her against the shaft, foot against the up ladder, but I knew she'd take me if she came from a height. So I waited a bit till her feet were above me."

Jethro had previously worked in coal at Nantyglo in Monmouthshire and he tells us that he hated this type of work which involved:

"... sixteen hour shifts six days a week, a shilling a day if the seam ran out, nothing if it ceased. Black trash were colliers these days. I had seen the battered heads of the Top Town colliers, the smashed hands of the hewing poor. Furnace work I do like if you can keep clear of the scald, but coal is a trap with no backdoor out. I cannot stand the galleries and the creak of the splintering prop. Drop the pick, go sideways, watch the slow lengthening of the wanene of the pole. Upward it spreads to the pitch, widening: ten million tons of mountain moving, perched on the tip of a four inch prop, and you hold your breath in the seconds of eternity while the County yawns and stretches in sunlight. For you, the microbe, work in the belly, raking at entrails, tunnelling in bowels, and the mountain growns as a child with an ache and its guts rumble thunder. It howls then as the wind breaks and seeks relief by changing position, then bucks to a bright explosion of pain, seeking the balm of its underground rivers. A hit in the stomach as its floor comes up; you squirm for protection as the roof comes down; grip, wait, ready for the crush."

From Kidwelly I followed the B4308 to cross the Gwendraeth Fawr, where I paused to examine an ancient bridge known as Pont Spwdwr. It is said to be the oldest surviving stone bridge in South Wales.

Further on I reached Trimsaron, an old mining village where I found a pub appropriately named *The Miners Arms*. In search of atmosphere and information about mining, I entered the bar.

Whilst enjoying a drink and a ham sandwich, I spoke to an old retired miner who coughed into his beer and told me with obvious sadness that the mines had all closed down many years ago.

At one time there were forty collieries operating in Carmarthenshire, and located in the Amman Valley were: Pontyffynon, Llandebie, Cross Hands, Tumble, Pontyberem, Llanelli, Trimsarn, Pontyates and Kidwelly. The coal mined was mainly anthracite.

The Miners Arms, Trimsaron

Llanelly owes its development and one time prosperity to coal mining, which began as long ago as 1540. The rich veins of coal beneath the town were known as "Rosy Vein", "Fiery Vein" and "Golden Vein". Carmarthen on the other hand was once famous for its weaving industry and the fine flannel produced there was in great demand.

The South Wales coalfield is an oval shaped basin, stretching nearly 90 miles from Pontypool in the east to Pembrokeshire in the west. Its width from north to south varies from 16 miles in the main part, to 4 miles in the detached part of the coalfield in South Pembrokeshire. There are three types of coal - bituminous, steam and anthracite, and it is the latter which occurs along the west and north edge of the coalfield.

On returning to Kidwelly I turned up the B4308, opposite the *White Lion Inn* and followed signs directing the way to the Kidwelly Industrial Museum, which is situated a couple of miles away on the banks of the Gwendraeth Fach. It is based on the site of Kidwelly Tinplate Works which were in operation until 1941. Originally it had been established in 1737 as an ironworks by Charles Gwynn, a gentleman of Kidwelly. It became the second tinplate works in Britain and the Gwendraeth Fach river provided the power to turn water wheels and drive the rolling mills.

Kidwelly Industrial Museum was originally a water powered mill. It is the site of an historic tin-plate works established in 1737 and is the only site in Wales where it is now possible to show how tin plate was made by hand.

Charles Gwynn had obtained his knowledge of tinplate processes from the Hanburys of Pontypool and he helped to lay the foundations on which the Welsh tinplate industry was established. In 1770 there were just five tinplate works in Britain, but by the middle of the nineteenth century, Britain had become the world's leading tinplate manufacturer.

Conversion of the works into a museum was begun in 1980 by volunteers, who two years later formed the Kidwelly Heritage Centre and this was officially opened in 1988 by Prince Charles.

Inside the museum, I first watched a video which told the story of the castle and the origins of Kidwelly and stressed its importance as an industrial centre and port. Production of tinplate commenced here in 1737 and this was the second tinplate works to be established in Britain. An area some twenty miles in length, from Kidwelly to Pontardulais, became the largest and the most important tinplate making area in the world. It was Jacob Chivers who really developed the works in the 1880s and his family home next door to the museum is now an hotel.

The video certainly gave me a fascinating insight into the techniques of tinplate making and the history of the works and the working conditions of the men and women employed here. It is important that the remains of this factory have been preserved to serve as a memorial to the tinplate industry and the generations of local people who once worked here.

At the far end of the site I found the coal museum which I hoped would provide me with some of the information that I was seeking and I was not disappointed. I learned that coal mining in this area extended for about 10 miles from the River Loughor in the east to the Gwendraeth Valley in the west.

The collieries along the Gwendraeth Fawr river were all anthracite and are all closed now. Since the 1950s mining was centred on the Cynheidre Colliery which was sunk to reach the deep productive coal seams while opencast mining had been carried out at Ffoslas. The workings in Cynheidre covered nearly 200 square miles and included about 146 miles of underground roadways. The last three seams to be mined were the Felin/Soap, Big and Pumpquart. Pentremawr Colliery, an old slant mine was connected to the Cynheidre complex until 1975 and was later used as a pumping station. Gas and underground water were a particular problem in Cynheidre with 10-15 million gallons of water a week being removed from the workings.

The Turnpike Trusts

"Things were happening in Carmarthenshire just now. The gentry were forming Trusts for road repairs and setting up toll gates to pay for the labour, but drawing hot profits for the money invested by charging the earth for tolls. Left and right the gates were going up now, placed to trap the small farmers. Graft, too, as usual, for some gentlemens' carriages passed the tollgates free and bridges were being built to serve the needs of the big houses. Men were flocking away from the land, queueing for the workhouses and at the beginning of Spring whole families were starving."

At this time the roads in Carmarthenshire were notorious at this time for their poor condition, with all maintenance being undertaken by the parishes. Every able-bodied man was required to do a minimum of one day per year on road repairing and this was obviously a very haphazard way of carrying out much needed repairs.

This system of compulsory labour was abolished by the Highways Act of 1835 and the responsibility for road improvements was given to a network of road Trusts. In order to obtain the necessary finance for repairing roads, these Trusts set up toll gates.

The very first Turnpike Trust had been set up in 1707 and the period 1750-70 saw the greatest expansion of turnpike roads. By the 1830s over 1,000 Turnpike Trusts were responsible for 225,000 miles (362,0292.5km) of road in England and Wales.

Twelve Turnpike Trusts were formed in Carmarthenshire, four in Pembrokeshire, two in Cardiganshire, one in Breconshire, and twelve in Glamorganshire. A turnpike road was so-called because at frequent intervals a gate or bar was placed across the road which would only be opened when the traveller had paid the toll.

The word 'turnpike' refers to swinging bars, tapered like a lance or pike and pivoted at the point of balance, which swung across the road on an upright post. Gates in due course replaced the swinging pikes. The person who looked after the gate and collected the tolls was a pikeman and he lived in a tollhouse beside the gate. The gates were placed at strategic points along roads leading into market towns.

Tollgates were particularly numerous in Carmarthenshire, and in one area there were eleven toll-bars on nineteen miles of road. By 1838 there were five different turnpike roads leading into Carmarthen alone, and a person travelling through the town in a particular direction had to pay at three turnpikes in a distance of three miles.

"Humble men and women, these keepers - the Welsh bleeding the Welsh, said Morfydd. The levying of the tolls was unjust, too, for some of the gentlemen's carriages passed free, because they were gentlemen; the charge for a horse and cart with broad wheels was fourpence while a cart with narrow wheels cost sixpence, so the richer the farmer the cheaper the toll."

For a time peace and good will appeared to prevail, but the numbers of toll gates increased at a rapid rate and farmers were now compelled to pay heavy taxes for the use of roads which had previously been maintained by themselves. The small farmers of Cardiganshire and Carmarthenshire often had to transport large quantities of lime for the fertilization of their land, over quite long distances and the tolls enforced on them were crippling. To redress their grievances, the farmers upon finding that their petitions were being ignored decided to form a league.

Tempers grew hot and secret meetings were held in West Carmarthenshire and East Pembrokeshire. It was agreed that such tyranny could no longer be tolerated and they decided to take action.

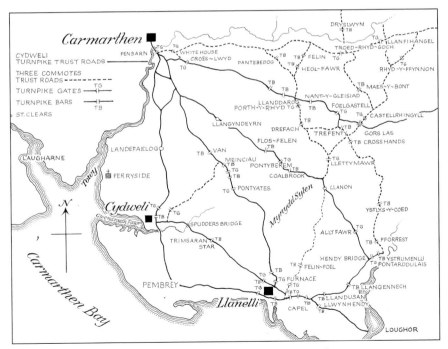

Turnpike Roads in the vicinity of Carmarthen

Birth of the Rebecca Movement

It was in the neighbourhood of Efailwen on the slopes of the Preseli Hills that the Rebecca movement was initially formed and the people of that district were also the first to appoint a leader.

At about 10.30 pm on 13th May, 1839, a band of some four hundred men attacked the new tollgate of the Whitland Trust at Efailwen within a week of its erection. Clothed in women's dresses, they had blackened faces and wore fern in their white caps. Their weapons consisted of sticks, pikes, spades, hatchets, old swords, guns; in fact anything they could obtain for the purpose.

Leading the band of rioters was Thomas Rees, a local farmer, who was better known as Twm Carnabwth. He was tall and powerfully built and this meant that great difficulty was experienced in finding a gown large enough to fit him. However, a dress belonging to a large stout lady named Rebecca, was discovered, and this with a few minor alterations became the leader's disguise. Twm was dubbed "Rebecca", and in due course leaders of other local riots adopted the same name.

In a very short time the Efailwen gate was pulled apart, chopped to pieces and then set on fire. The gatekeeper and his family were forced to run off into the nearby fields. Their work done, the mob then disappeared silently into the blackness of the night. This was the start of a long series of similar actions and the Rebecca movement was firmly established. It was shortly afterwards that these Bible-bred countrymen decided to make use of a few words from the appropriate sixth verse of Chapter 24 in Genesis:

> "And they blessed Rebecca, and said unto her, Thou art our sister, be thou the mother of thousands of millions, and let thy seed possess the gate of those which hate them."

These are the words of Labon, which he spoke to Rebecca when she was leaving her father's house to go to Jacob. The Rebecca leaders were able to persuade their followers that these words from the Bible were nothing less than a command from God for them to destroy the hated gates.

Their activities did not always involve the destruction of tollgates, for they also took it upon themselves to punish folk who in their eyes had been guilty of misbehaviour. Those who deserved punishment were visited at night by local men dressed in womens' clothes. They carried with them an effigy of the offender sitting on a wooden horse and this was burnt in front of his home. Sometimes the man would be beaten as well, if his crime was thought to merit such punishment.

GYPERBYN AR GARREG
HON ARY BEG O FAI
1839 Y DINISTRIWID
TOLLBORTH AR Y FFORDD
DYRPEG AM Y TRO
CYNTAF A THRWY
HYNNY DECHREUWYD
RHYDDHAU FFYRDD
Y WLAD

This plaque beside the A478 at Efailwen was erected in 1964 and it records an attack made on the tollgate here on the evening of Whit Monday, 13 May 1839. It was led by Thomas Rees of Mynachlog-ddu. The plaque was unveiled by the historian David Williams and it shows Thomas Rees, robed as a Rebecca, astride his horse and wielding an axe as he leads the charge on the gate.

The Whitland Trust immediately replaced the Efailwen gate with a new one, which was made of wood plated with iron, so as to prevent it being cut down with hatchets and saws. Special constables were sent to Efailwen to guard the gate, but it was not long before Rebecca and her daughters returned and the 'specials' fled in fear of their lives, while the gate was destroyed once more.

In due course each district had its own Rebecca, who planned the various enterprises and was the undisputed leader of the gang, which was sometimes over two hundred strong. They would assemble at different locations for a quick briefing from the leader and then set off into the night, mainly mounted on horses, to attack and destroy a selected turnpike-gate. When they arrived at the gate a preliminary ritual would take place. The leader would ask his followers:

"My daughters, this gate has no business here, has it?"

The men replied shouting "No!" in unison. Then the gate would be destroyed and the occupants of the tollhouse ejected from their home which would be set on fire.

Rebecca Rioters destroying a gate

"Up and down the country the gates were going up in flames, with scores of Rebeccas and hundreds of men riding every night, winning the race of building and burning. Magistrates were shivering in their beds, horses of the dragoons dropping dead in the fruitless gallops after Rebecca; lost in the maze of a country we knew backwards, redirected, misdirected, laughed to scorn, publicly insulted. The military heads were being recalled and replaced, the military stations were strengthened, all to no avail. Rebecca grew as an army in numbers. The Trusts were being defeated, and knew it."

One gate, at the *Mermaid Tavern,* just outside St Clears was only in place for a matter of hours before Rebecca came in the darkness and destroyed it. In fact it was not long before all the gates owned by the Whitland and the Tavernspite Trusts were destroyed.

At about midnight on 7th April 1843, Rebecca and a number of her offspring arrived at Bwlchtrap near St Clears and the following conversation between Rebecca and her daughters, is typical of the play acting that took place, just before a gate was destroyed.

Rebecca, leaning on her staff would hobble up to the gate and appear very surprised that her progress along the road was blocked.

Rebecca:	"Children, there is something put here. I cannot go on."
Daughters:	"What is it mother? Nothing should be in your way."
Rebecca:	"I do not know, children, I am old and cannot see well."
Daughters:	"Shall we come on mother, and move it out of the way?"
Rebecca:	"Stop, let me see first. It seems like a great gate, put across the road to stop your old mother."
Daughters:	"We will break it mother. Nothing shall hinder you on your journey."
Rebecca:	"No, let me see, perhaps it will open. No children, it is bolted and locked, and I cannot go on. What is to be done?"
Daughters:	"It must be taken down mother, because you and your children must pass."
Rebecca:	"Off with it, then children. It has no business here."

All the 'children' would then set about destroying the gate, and within about ten minutes not a vestige of the gate or posts would remain. The band of rioters would then disappear into the night.

Rebecca leading the toll-gate rioters

One of the most serious of these incidents occurred on the 19th June 1843. Rebecca had issued orders that all males between the ages of sixteen and seventy should assemble at the *Plough and Harrow*, an inn two miles from Carmarthen, under pain of having their houses burnt and their lives sacrificed. A great force assembled at the rendezvous, and in spite of the entreaties of influential local men, they marched into Carmarthen, armed with cudgels.

The mob consisted of some 4000 men on foot and nearly 500 on horseback, many of them disguised as women. An attack was made on the Union Workhouse. The master and matron were compelled to surrender their keys, and in the board-room, some of the rioters danced upon the table. Just at this moment the dragoons appeared and the Rebeccaites fled in all directions. Several were arrested and order was finally restored.

> *"The whole teeming countryside from coast to coast brawled and rioted into open revolution. Special constables were sworn in to protect the gates, special constables were dragged out and horse-whipped by the Rebeccas. The dragoons and marines were dashing around arresting people, the magistrates had special sittings, with public warnings and transportations; the prisons were crammed to their doors, workhouses bulging. From Whitland to Laugharne, Saundersfoot to Carmarthen, the yeoman farmers armed for the fight."*

On Friday 25th August 1843, a massive meeting was held on the slopes of Mynydd Sylen. It was attended by 3,000 people, consisting mainly of farmers and colliers who all forfeited a day's pay in order to attend. The chairman was William Chambers Junior of Llanelli and the main item on the agenda was to consider a list of grievances, which had been prepared by Hugh Williams, a solicitor who many later believed to have been the mysterious mastermind behind the Rebecca riots. He spoke for a considerable time, and after much discussion the list of complaints was adopted. In due course a petition was submitted to Queen Victoria.

The petition complained that the turnpike tolls were too heavy; it suggested that all Turnpike Trusts should be consolidated under one management, and the distances between the gates could thereafter be fixed at regular intervals; it asserted that the new Poor Law was too heavy in its demands upon the parishes, and the petitioners prayed that the old Poor Law should be restored; the old tithes, paid in money or in kind, according to option, should be restored; legal and magisterial fees were exorbitant; stipendary magistrates should replace the Commission of the Peace, as the latter were actuated by class motives and were the nominees of party and moneyed interests; rentals should be assessed, and all tithes and local taxes should be charged on the land and not on the tenant; the present Parliament, having shown its utter lack of sympathy with the demands and needs of the masses, should be dismissed by the Queen, and a new Parliament more in conformity with the wishes of the nation should be summoned in its place.

After the meeting had finished the crowd dispersed and many of the men went drinking in the local inns. One in particular, Shoni Sguberfawr (alias John Jones) got very drunk and went berserk. He was later seen wandering around Pontyberem dressed in a petticoat loudly proclaiming that he was Becca. He shot one man who argued with him and chased him into the *New Inn*, where he fired at a man named Walter Rees. The landlord then managed to throw him out and lock the door, but Shoni returned soon afterwards and drank a quart of beer.

In due course the law caught up with him and he was subsequently sentenced and transported for life.

Thomas Rees the first leader to be called Rebecca

In the village of Mynachlog-ddu in the heart of the Preseli Hills, I visited Bethel Chapel in search of the grave of Thomas Rees, who was the first leader to be known as *Rebecca*, when the Efailwen tollgate was attacked in May 1839. More than a century of erosion by the elements had made the original tombstone impossible to read and in recent years it has been replaced by a new one, thus giving recognition to Thomas Rees as a local man of historical importance.

New headstone marking the grave of Thomas Rees

The Welsh inscription reads:

Er cof am
Thomas Rees, Trial
Mynachlogddu:
Bu farw Tachwedd 17eg 1876
Yn 70 mlwydd oed.
Nid oes neb ond Duw yn gwybod
Beth a ddigwydd mewn diwarnod;
Wrth gyrchu bresych at fy nghinio
Daeth angeu i fy ngardd i'm taro.

("No one but God knows what may happen
in one day. While fetching a cabbage for my
dinner, death came into my garden and struck me.")

Thomas Rees was known as "Twm Carnabwth" (Tom Stonecottage) because he resided at 'Carnbwth', a tiny cottage that he built at Glynsaithmaen Farm, on the lower slope of Foel Cwmcerwyn. He raised this dwelling on the ancient 'squatter's right', a tradition known as Ty Unnos ('a one night house'), which allowed the owner of a building erected overnight, the right of occupancy, provided that smoke could be seen issuing from its chimney by the following morning.

Here, Thomas Rees lived with his wife Rachel and their children, Elizabeth, Daniel and John, in a single room measuring 20 feet by 12 feet. The ruins of this cottage can be seen on the bank of a tributary to the Cleddau, at the foot of Preseli Top (GR 119305).

He was employed as a farm labourer and in 1839 was about 36 years of age. Strongly built and handy with his fists he had a reputation as a local pugilist, who lost one eye while prize fighting. He was rather fond of his beer, but was also a regular chapel goer and knew his Bible well.

As a Rebecca leader, Thomas Rees certainly distinguished himself and succeeded in destroying many tollgates. Most of his followers wore betgowns (the peasant dress of Welsh women), and were frequently called Mary, Jane, or Nelly, after the names of the women whose gowns they wore. "Rebecca" pretended to be the mother and the others were her "daughters"; and they addressed each other as such when attacking the tollgates.

After the riots came to an end, Thomas Rees continued his hold over the district in which he lived, and whenever a pugulist visited the place, he was always put up as champion and invariably gave a good account of himself.

On 17th November, 1876, at the age of seventy years, he was found dead in the garden adjoining his own house. It is believed that his death was caused by a fit of apoplexy or a stroke while gathering vegetables for dinner.

The March on Carmarthen

"This very morning Rebecca was marching on Carmarthen, but I was sick of fighting. Led by Rebecca John Harries of Talog Mill, thousands of the daughters were marching on the city to burn the workhouse down, they said; burn it to the ground and succour the starving and God help the man who stands in our path."

On 19th June, 1843, a large mob of Rebecca rioters assembled at 11.00am at the *Plough and Harrow Inn*, near Newchurch and then marched through the ruins of Water Street gate. About 500 men on horseback followed the leader and behind them came about 2,000 men on foot.

They carried a big white banner bearing the words, 'CYFIAWNDER A CHARWYR CYFIAWNDER'. This translates, 'Justice, and lovers of justice are we all.'

Other banners bore such statements as 'RHYDDID A GWELL LLUNIAETH' ('Freedom and better food'), and TOLL RYDD A RHYDDID ('Free tolls and Freedom').

The mob made their way into Carmarthen and attacked the workhouse but the 4th Light Dragoons arrived from Cardiff and pursued them with drawn sabres. The Rebeccaites were scattered in all directions and some of them were trapped in the workhouse courtyard, where they were taken prisoner.

Lieutenant Rees Jones wrote the following report:

"They arrived at Carmarthen about noon, marching four or five abreast. The procession reached from the gaol through Spilman Street, Church Street, St Peter's Street, to the King Street end of Conduit Lane and numbered from 2,000 to 2,500 persons. A man disguised with long hair rode in front on a rather low horse. It is believed that at first there was no intention to commit excesses, and that the country people were led to the workhouse by some town roughs. Others maintain that the attack on the workhouse was deliberately resolved on at the meeting held the previous Wednesday at Talog and other places. Be that as it may, to the workhouse they went. The dragoons were expected earlier than they arrived, having, it is said, been mis-directed by a countryman whom they met between Pontarddulais and Carmarthen. They came just in time to save the workhouse and possibly the neighbouring brewery, the contents of which might have given further impulse to the fury of the rioters."

At the end of July 1843, Mr Hall, the Chief Magistrate of Bow Street Police Office, was sent to Wales to inquire into the circumstances connected with the riots.

In August *The Times* sent Thomas Campbell Foster, a special commisioner to Carmarthenshire, to report upon the riots and their causes. He won the confidence of the farmers and the grievances he learned of were made public. The following is an extract from *The Times*, August 1843:

"The farmers loudly complain of the oppressive nature of the tolls, particularly on those roads, originally parish roads, and which the trust adopted, placed turnpikes on them, and then called on the Parishes to keep them in repair. They gave me an instance of a parish road between Llanelly and Pymbrae, a distance of five miles, on which a gate has been erected, and a sixpenny toll demanded for a horse and cart. A fortnight ago a bridge on this road was broken down by a flood. The trustees refused to do anything, and called on the parish to repair it. They say that there is not a by-lane of any sort by which a cart can get to the lime-kilns which has not a bar or a chain across it. They say if ever there is a lane by which one or two farmers can get to their farm without paying tolls, an application is immediately made to the trustees to grant a bar on the lane, which is almost always of course acceded to; that there is never a fair held in any of the villages or principal towns but the toll contractor surrounds the town by every approachable access to it with a cordon of toll bars. Chains are fastened across the roads close to towns, and thus they catch every farmer who has cattle, or sheep, or horses, or carts to bring to the fair. This is done sometimes by the licence of the trustees, but in very many cases they say that these chains are put across the lanes, and toll demanded by the contractor, without any licence whatever. By many of these lanes, by going a mile or two round, the farmers could escape toll. The lanes are kept in repair by the parishes, and are many of them quite as good as the high roads of the trusts. The trust extends over 71 miles of roads of all descriptions, and on these roads and lanes there are 15 bars and 14 gates at which toll is demanded - that is 29 turnpikes, or a turnpike for about every two miles and a half. Of course some of these turnpikes clear others, but still it is impossible for a farmer to stir two miles from home in any direction without having a bar or gate to pay toll at. This, with the fact that many of these roads are maintained by themselves, naturally has greatly exasperated them, and the toll bars and gates are continually being demolished."

On 6th September 1843, a group of men led by John Hughes, a young farmer, known locally as Jac Ty Isha attacked the Pontardulais gate, but they were ambushed by the recently formed Glamorgan Police who fired muskets on them and they dispersed. However, Jac Ty Isha and two of his followers were captured.

A few days later on the 9th September, the Hendy gate was attacked by the 'Stag and Pheasant Gang.' On this occasion the gate-keeper, Sarah Williams, was murdered and consequently public opinion was reversed, for the rioters had gone too far. An informer gave the names of the leaders and before long Shoni Sguborfawr (John of the Great Granary) and Dai'r Cantwr (Dai the Singer) were arrested.

Shoni Sguborfawr was about 32 years of age and born in Merthyr Tydfil. He took his name from the farm, Sgubor-fawr, in the neighbourhood of Pendern, where he had probably been employed as a labourer. He became a prizefighter, and when the Taff Vale Railway was opened to Merthyr in 1840, the event was celebrated by a bare-fist encounter between Shoni and John Nash, the champion of Cyfarthfa. Soon afterwards, depression in the iron trade at Merthyr drove him westwards in search of work.

"I drew my breath at the sight of his face. It was ravaged, with the flattened features of the mountain fighter. Bull-necked, mop haired, grinning, this one, and his clothes were ragged, his shirt open to the waist despite the frosty night and his feet and legs were bare, his ragged gentry riding breeches tied at the knees. Shoni Sgubor Fawr. This was the trash that was hanging a stink on the name of Rebecca..."

Dai'r Cantwr was born in Llancarfan in the Vale of Glamorgan, the son of a tenant-farmer. He had been a farm labourer and a quarryman as well as an industrial worker at Tredegar in Monmouthshire. He came to Pontyberem in search of employment and acted as a middleman between pit-owners and a number of workmen. However, he appeared to be unemployed during the brief time when he took part in the Rebecca Riots. He is said to have been a poet and a ballad singer whose songs were about the events of that time.

The two men talked their heads off whilst in prison and betrayed all their followers. On 27th December, they were both sentenced at the Guildhall, Carmarthen to transportation for twenty years.

Before this incident, the magistrates had found it very difficult to track down the ringleaders of the Rebecca movement, for the local people were all sworn to secrecy and would not divulge any information, for fear of their lives.

St Clears

I found St Clears to be much larger than I expected and it was obviously once a place of some importance, being a port on the river Tâf at its confluence with the Gynin. The name comes from "Santa Clara", who founded a simple church here in the sixth century. Five hundred years later, the Normans arrived and built a castle where the mound known as "Banc y brili" can be seen. It was no doubt built there to guard the entrance to the two river valleys.

The *Black Lion* in St Clears was used for Rebecca meetings

St Clears was of particular interest to me, for it was once the main headquarters of the Rebecca movement and the *Black Lion Hotel* in the main street was used for meetings. Outside this building is an old metal milestone inscribed '9 miles to Carmarthen 1839'. Thus it was set up in the very same year that the first attack on the tollgate at Efailwen took place. Soon after this historic event, members of the Whitland Trust met at the *Blue Boar Inn* at St Clears to consider the worrying situation.

Near the *Black Lion Inn* is a very fine wood carving representing some Rebecca rioters destroying a tollgate and it commemorates the attack on the *Mermaid Tavern* Gate.

This metal milestone in St Clears was erected in 1839. The Turnpike Trusts were responsible for erecting milestones along their routes and many trusts had distinctive designs. They were usually made of cast iron and often V-shaped to make them easy to read.

This remarkable carving depicting some Rebecca rioters destroying a toll gate can be seen in the centre of St Clears, near the *Black Lion Hotel*.

Hugh Williams, Carmarthen Attorney, may have been the organiser of the Rebecca movement.

It is of interest that the Chartist leader Hugh Williams (1796 -1874) once lived in St Clears and became Mayor of the town. Whilst being opposed to the violent ways of the Rebecca rioters, he drew up petitions relating to their demands and helped to defend men who were captured.

Hugh Williams was originally from Machynlleth and he came to Carmarthen as a solicitor. He organised the first Radical meeting in South Wales at Carmarthen, which was celebrated by a huge crowd of 4,000 carrying torches around Picton's monument. In addition he formed the first branch of the Working Men's Association in Carmarthen. He married a lady from St Clears and came to live at the property she owned here at 'Gardde' some time before 1851. In that year, he became port-reeve of St Clears, and he and his wife built a market hall in the town, and tried without much success to establish a market there. He became recorder of St Clears in 1853 and, despite several protests after 1867, on account of his absence from the borough, retained the office until his death.

His wife, Anne Jones was twenty-five years his senior and died at Llanfihangel Abercywyn on 5th August 1861 in her ninetieth year.

Hugh Williams re-married two months later and his new wife, Elizabeth Anthony of Llan-saint, was thirty-nine years younger than he was. They went to live in Ferryside where they had four children. He died on 19 October 1874, in his seventy-eighth year, at Cobden Villa, Ferryside, and is buried in the churchyard of St Ishmaels.

St Ishmael's Church, Ferryside

Grave of Hugh Williams
St Ishmael's Churchyard, Ferryside

Before taking action, Rebecca usually sent a note to her victim informing him or her of a coming attack. The notes were written on cheap paper and in an illiterate hand, although there is reason to believe, owing to the legal and political information which they contain, that at times they were the composition of a learned man who sought to disguise his identity under a cloak of illiteracy.

Hugh Williams may well have been the leading figure behind the organisation of the Rebecca Riots in West Wales and William James Linton, writing in 1895, makes the following statement:

> "Hugh Williams, the Carmarthen Lawyer, a man of large business till he lost favour by his defence of poor men, was the instigator and undiscovered leader of the Rebecca Movement.
>
> I dined with him one evening and he sent me off to Pontyberem, where next day was to be a gathering in favour of universal suffrage, a step beyond the toll gate movement, which Williams from the first had meant as a preparation for further political action."

It was near St Clears that Jethro killed a trooper in a nearby wood.

> *"The soldier rode up, dismounted, tied his horse and approached the wood. Cool customer, this one, though few Rebeccas were armed save with useless powder-guns. He took his time; a big man, over six feet, with the pistol lying in his palm. Castlemartin Yeomanry by the look of him, a long way from home and dying for the skin of the hated Rebecca."*

> *"Right, you bloody swine Rebecca," he gasped, and dived at my legs, but I leapt away and he went past sprawling, and waited for the next time. Big as a horse he looked in that moonlight, confident, trained to a hair with his yeomanry service; not much older than me by the look of him; farmer probably, I remember thinking - farmer fighting farmer, gentry against the people. "*

> *"Fighting for life. I measured him, sighted the chin and hit it crisply, and he clutched at the tree and went down it slowly, rolled over once and lay still at my feet. With my hands to my face I swayed above him. I do not remember him catching me square, but there was blood on my fingers when I drew him clear. Gasping, I leaned against the tree above him with the world of moonlight spinning above me, with no sound but the bluster of wind and the gasping breaths of the soldier below me. I got to the brook and knelt in the water, letting the coldness flood over me, bringing back life."*

It is interesting that in Newcastle Emlyn Churchyard can be seen the grave of trooper John Kearns, 4th Light Dragoons, who was involved in dealing with the attack on Carmarthen Workhouse. His epitaph reads:

"He fell not in the battle strife, nor on the sultry plain.
Death did not meet the Warrior there, nor on the stormy main.
But there, in Tivy's winding stream, on a sunny summer's day,
where bating peacefully he sank, his spirit passed away.
Mourn reader, with his comrades mourn o'er one so young
and brave, and trust in Him whose mighty arm from
endless death can save."

Grave of Trooper John Kearns, 4th Light Dragoons, in Newcastle Emlyn Churchyard. His death occured one week after taking part in dealing with the attack on the Carmarthen Workhouse.

The End of the Tollgates

In due course the trustees lost heart and stopped replacing the tollgates and toll houses which left the roads free from toll charges.

"The Trusts had lost all heart for rebuilding and the splintered remains of gates littered the highways, the charred timbers of the toll-house rafters grinning at the summer sky."

On the 7th November 1843, a Royal Commission was appointed to inquire into the grievances of the peasantry of West Wales. It was found that there was substantial ground for disaffection, and the suggestions of the Commissioners were embodied in the Act of 1844 which amended the Turnpike Trusts Act and removed many of the problems which had given rise to the Rebecca riots. The several Trusts in each of the respective counties were consolidated and placed under uniform management and control, and the laws and regulations relating to the collection and application of tolls were revised and amended.

The removal of the most burdensome of their grievances brought the Rebecca Riots to an end. As the agitation against the Truck Act was successful in removing the Truck System from the industrial districts of Wales, so the Rebecca Riots removed the most unjust impositions of the Turnpike Trusts, and did much to liberate commerce by the removal of onerous tolls and dues.

In due course County Road Boards were created and Local Authorities made responsible for roads. The last tollgate in Britain was removed from Llanfairpwll, Anglesey, in October 1895.

Jethro Sails from Saundersfoot

"I knew of a ship at Saundersfoot; a three-masted barque that was lying at the quay; waiting for the flood of immigrants from the north - people coming down on foot, it was said. Two weeks or longer she had laid at Saundersfoot with her sails trimmed down and smoke from her galleys, and her captain was taking the fares at the gang-plank, five pounds a head steerage, fifteen pounds a head cabins. Bound for the port of Philadelphia: a leap from there to the town of Pittsburgh and the flaming ovens of the iron."

"I would hang in her rigging, unfurl her sails, tar her from bow to stern while she rode at sea, scrub her white, labour in the galleys,

bow and scrape to the dining gentry - just to hear the song of her, feel the roll of her, the buck and toss of the swell beneath her and listen to the whine of the Atlantic gales that drove her west to Philadelphia. ... I had to get away."

"What is it that enters the blood and chains a man's soul to the soul of his country? What is it that pierces as a barb and cannot be drawn? O, this beloved country that has raised its sword to the fire of its persecutors and reddened its soil with beloved sons! Wales! What lies in your possession that you bite at the throats of those who leave you? You of the mountainous crags of Dinas, of Snowdon, Pembrey and Capel Pass - you of the valleys, heaths and pastures, the roaring rivers, the village brooks - what is your golden key that turns in the hearts of your patriots; what flame sears their souls in the last goodbye."

Jethro sails to America from Saundersfoot Harbour

Jethro departs to America, escaping from the long arm of the law and in search of a new life. Mari Mortymer is left behind at Cae White and is now on her own, having been told that her husband Iestyn was killed trying to escape whilst being taken to Monmouth Gaol with other Chartist prisoners.

We meet Mari again in Cordell's next book *Song of the Earth* and she is the last of the Mortymer family to feature in his trilogy. I once suggested to Cordell that he should continue the story of Jethro by bringing him back from America in search of his family. But Alex immediately shook his head and said, "No, I never really liked Jethro for he was a weak character and I have done with him."

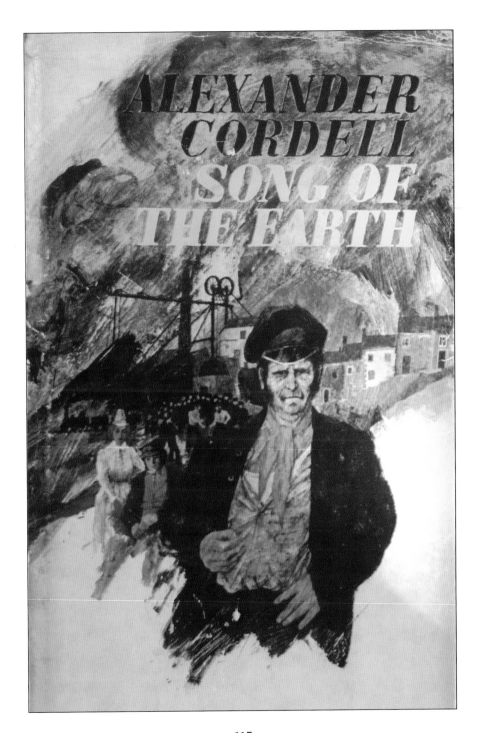

SONG OF THE EARTH

'A meaty novel, full of characters and incidents. A lurid, violent world of tommy shops, starving and exploited Irish, revivalist religion and early revolutionary politics is sketched with complete mastery. As a historian of this period Mr Cordell can have few equals.'

The Times

This third part of Cordell's trilogy was first published in 1989 and is set in the industrial era of the first half of the 19th century. It tells the story of a fictitious family who came from a long line of colliers, but decided to become boatmen, working the Neath Canal.

It seems an idyllic way of earning a living, but the livelihood of the canal workers is suddenly threatened, for a railway is being constructed through the Neath Valley, by the famous engineer Isambard Kingdom Brunel and life for the boatmen will never be the same again.

Cordell's tale is full of humour, drama, vivid description and sadness, providing an enthralling mixture that is so typical of all his novels set in the Welsh Valleys.

The story begins in Merthyr Tydfil in the winter of 1845 and it is told by Bryn, the youngest son of Mostyn Evan. His brothers are the twins Dewi and Ifor and his sisters are Gwen and Sharon. Their mother has just passed away and is being taken away in a cart for burial at Vaynor.

A year later, Bryn starts work with his father and two brothers at Cyfarthfa. They are employed as hauliers, taking boat loads of iron down to the Abercynon Basin on the Glamorgan Canal, which runs from Merthyr to Cardiff.

"Down to the Basin with us then, with the crippled trees flaring at a leaden sky: a blue-eared morning, this one, with the hedges dripping icicles and the ice-breakers labouring up the canals and the big Carmarthen drays skidding their hooves down the tow-path, breaking it up. Aye, a wicked old winter this one, and now well into March."

"On through Quakers Yard, on to Abercynon, the clearing house of iron for the world. Here the great warehouses and offices where half-starved clerks were bending over ledgers: on down the brick cut and the fields where the little children laboured on the frosted land; on to Lock One, the most important in the Basin."

"On, on to the loading wharves where hundreds of horses were towing trams heaped with the coal and iron of the Top Towns, and as we drew closer to the Basin platforms the explosions of iron-making grew about us; great rainbows of light flooding over the skies above Hirwaun and Aberdare. It was the firework display of the mountains; the music of the Crawshays and Guests, the Hills of Plymouth, the Foremans of Penydarren."

The Glamorganshire Canal

Before the development of transport systems the ouput of the ironworks in Merthyr Tydfil, consisting largely of pig iron, had to be carried down the Taff Valley on horseback or on carts, to the port of Cardiff about 25 miles away. This was most unsatisfactory and it was soon realised that the only way forward was to build a canal. Compared to the hundredweight or so which a horse could carry, the canal barges could transport an impressive 25 tons of iron.

The construction of a canal 24.5 miles long down the Taff Valley was authorised by the Act of 1790 and the engineer-contractors who were appointed to build it were Thomas Dadford Senior, his son Thomas and Thomas Sheasby. It was constructed at a cost of £103,600, to which Samuel Homfray subscribed £40,000. Most of the shares were subsequently bought by Richard Crawshay, the 'Iron King' of Cyfarthfa.

This was the first major canal in Wales and a noted engineering feat of its day. On Friday February 7th 1794 a fleet of canal boats from Merthyr laden with iron completed the journey to Cardiff. The first barge was 'finely decorated with colours'.

There were 49 locks in its 24.5 miles from the head of the canal at Cyfarthfa, 568 feet above sea level and a 115 yard tunnel at Cardiff. A lock at Aberfan had a fall of 14 feet 6 inches which made it the deepest lock on any British canal.

Not only were the chambers of the fifty-two locks on this canal unusually deep, but they also included no less than eleven pairs of double locks and one triple staircase below Nantgarw. Such a concentration of locks is unique in Britain.

This was the most important canal in South Wales for it provided an outlet for the four ironworks in the neighbourhood of Merthyr: Dowlais, Cyfarthfa, Penydarren and Plymouth, names famous in the history of the Industrial Revolution.

The canal head at Cyfarthfa is 568 feet above sea level which is the highest level reached by any major canal in Wales. The canal was fed by the river Taff which once flowed through the site of the Cyfartha Ironworks.

In addition, ironworks and collieries in the neighbourhood of Aberdare, Dyffryn and Mountain Ash were tapped when the independently promoted Aberdare Canal, running down the Cynon Valley for seven miles to join the Glamorganshire at Abercynon, was completed in 1812. The Aberdare Canal was proposed by Thomas Dadford in 1800:

> "I recommend cutting a canal from the Glamorganshire Canal, at the head of the 7th lock above the Aqueduct over the river Taff, to a place called Ty Draw, nearly opposite Aberdare Village, which will be 7 miles in length, with a rise of nearly 25 feet, and wanting about 12 bridges, and I estimate the same, all expenses included, at Ten Thousand Five Hundred Pounds.
> From this Canal to the Furnaces, I propose a Tramroad one mile and a half in length, which I estimate at One Thousand Five Hundred Pounds, including every expense."

Sadly, the Aberdare canal now lies beneath the B4275 and A4059 roads.

By 1830 the Glamorganshire canal was carrying more than 200 thousand tons of coal and iron per year and the tolls charged were 2d a ton per mile for coal, ironstone, limestone, iron ore, lime, manure, sand, clay and bricks; 5d a ton per mile for iron, timber and general merchandise. The boats working the Glamorganshire Canal were 60 feet long by 8 feet 6 inches beam and could carry 20 tons on a draft of 2 feet 9 inches. The horse towing mast was 6 feet high.

In order to allow night working, the locks in 1836 were lit by gas and oil lamps and by this time there were over 200 barges working the canal. The haulage time from one end of the canal to the other was about 20 hours and they generally did three round trips a fortnight.

Abercynon

Abercynon developed as an important junction of the Glamorganshire and Aberdare Canals and the Penydarren tramroad. Cottages were built initially around the basin area, where boats were unloaded to use the Penydarren tram road to Merthyr, or wait their turn to ascend through the long lock system.

Navigation House (ST 085948) was built by Thomas Dadford as a result of a decision made at a meeting of the Glamorganshire Canal Company on 25th September 1790, when it was minuted:

> "It being deemed necessary that a House shall be built on Craig Evan Leyshon near the Aqueduct for the use of the Proprietors, the expense of which shall not exceed £100. Mr Cockshutt shall settle the plan and contract for building such a House as soon as possible."

Thomas Dadford completed the building by 1792 and he resided there whilst constructing the canal. It served as the canal company's headquarters until the 1880s when the office was transferred to Cardiff. It then became the *Navigation Inn* which is still in use today.

From Abercynon Basin the canal crossed the river Taff on an aqueduct to follow its east bank to Cardiff for 15 miles. Above the aqueduct the canal rose 207 feet in one mile, through a series of sixteen locks to reach Cefn Glas (ST 086950 to ST 087956).

The Penydarren Tramroad (also known as the Merthyr Tramroad) was constructed using a clause in the Glamorganshire Canal Act which allowed roadways to be constructed within 4 miles of the canal to convey goods to it. The tramway was started in 1800 with Richard Hill of Plymouth Ironworks responsible for the overall direction of the project.

Navigation House at Abercynon, dating from 1791, was the administrative centre of the Glamorganshire Canal Co. for almost a century. It was also the site of the Company's maintenance yard, sawpit and dry dock. The building became a public house in 1890 which is still open today.

This memorial to Richard Trevethick can be seen in Merthyr(SO 052067). It commemorates his famous Penydarren locomotive which was the world's first steam locomotive to run on rails, when on 21st February 1804, it hauled a train to Navigation on the Merthyr Tramroad.

Reconstruction of the southern portal of the Merthyr Tramroad Tunnel on the site of the Plymouth Works (SO 057045).

Mural inside the southern portal of the Merthyr Tramroad Tunnel commemorating Trevethick's famous locomotive.

Cordell refers to the historic event in 1804 when the famous Cornish engineer Richard Trevethick used a steam powered locomotive to pull trams along the Penydarren Tramroad.

A wager was agreed by Samuel Homfray with Richard Crawshay that Trevethick's locomotive, which had been made in his own ironworks, could haul a load of 10 tons of iron from Merthyr to Abercynon. It was a distance of 9 miles and the empty trucks had to be hauled back. Each party deposited a stake of 500 guineas with Richard Hill, proprietor of the Plymouth Ironworks.

On February 22nd 1804, Trevethick wrote:

> "Yesterday we proceeded on our journey with the engine; we carry'd ten tons of Iron, five wagons, and 70 men riding on them the whole of the journey. It's above 9 miles which we perform'd in 4 hours and 5 mints, but we had to cut down some trees and remove large rocks out of the road. The engine, while working, went nearly 5 miles per hour, there was no water put into the boiler from the time we started until we arriv'd at our journey's end. The coal consumed was 2 Hund'd. On our return home abt 4 miles from the shipping place of the iron, one of the small bolts that fastened the axle to the boiler broak, and let all the water out of the boiler, which prevented the engine returning until this evening."

At one point on the outward journey the locomotive's chimney stack, which was made of bricks collapsed when it hit a bridge. But undeterred, Trevethick rebuilt it and continued on his way.

The original engine only made three more trips. It broke down and was then used as a stationary engine and it is believed that it was buried under the slag heaps of Penydarren. Trevethick never received the credit his many inventions deserved and suffered misfortune throughout his career. He died in poverty in 1833.

Of interest is Trevethick's Tunnel which passed right underneath the charging area of the Plymouth Ironworks (so called because the land was leased from the Earl of Plymouth). The tunnel was 8 feet high and 8 feet wide and in the reconstructed entrance can be seen an ornamental mosaic which celebrates the historic rail journey made on 21st February 1804 when Trevethick's engine, harnessed to five wagons, containing a total of 10 tons of iron, travelled from Penydarren to Navigation House at Abercynon.

But Trevethick's locomotive had proved unreliable and the iron rails of the tramroad broke too easily under the weight of the engine and the wagons. It was some years before a better quality iron for stronger rails became available.

The *Quakers Yard Inn* was established in 1742 and it was here that Joseph Bailey, when just a boy in search of his fortune, having walked all the way from Yorkshire, arrived with no shoes. He encountered Wayne and Knowles, the two managers of the Cyfarthfa Ironworks and asked to be directed to Mr Richard Crawshay. On revealing that Crawshay was his uncle, Joseph was given a meal and then taken in their trap to Cyfarthfa where his wealthy relation was delighted to see him. Joseph was given a job, starting at the bottom of the iron trade and in due course became manager of the works and his uncle's right hand man. The rest is history for he ultimately became a baronet and landed gentleman at Glanusk, near Crickhowell.

Richard Crawshay (1739-1810) was the chief promoter and shareholder of the Glamorganshire Canal. He was known as the 'Iron King' and founded a dynasty of ironmasters who passed on the business to their sons for several generations. By all accounts Richard Crawshay was a popular man who treated his workers well. He died in 1810 and is buried in Llandaff Cathedral.

The Taff Valley Railway was the first to be built in Wales and Sir Josiah Guest of Dowlais was the prime mover with the support of Samuel Homfray and Anthony Hill. Negotiations began with the renowned engineer Isambard Kingdom Brunel who made a report on the proposals. He estimated the cost of building a railway from Merthyr Tydfil to Cardiff would be £190,649.

In 1836 the Act of Parliament was given Royal Assent and the capital fixed for the venture was £300,000 divided into £100 shares. The first chairman of the Taff Vale Railway was Sir John Josiah Guest of Dowlais. Work began to construct a one track line between Navigation, Abercynon and Cardiff, a distance of fifteen miles, and it opened in October 1840. In 1841 it was extended to Merthyr Tydfil making a total distance of just under 25 miles. The railway was allowed to carry goods and passengers, the fare being no more than 1 ½d per mile and the maximum speed was set at 12mph.

By 1870 the Taff Valley Railway was taking away most of the business from the canal and in 1898 the Merthyr section was closed, because it had problems with subsidence caused by mining.

John Lloyd, author of *The Early History of the Old South Wales Ironworks*, who came here in 1906 expressed his surprise that the canal:

> "... had fallen into complete disuse, not a vestige of a canal boat was to be seen, and the water supply turned off into the river! Very little more than one hundred years have been long enough to bring about this marvellous change from high dividends and great prosperity to absolute ruin... and on the day of my visit the water in the lock was green and stagnant, and the massive lock gates had not apparently turned upon their hinges for months past!"

The Abercynon-Pontypridd section closed in 1915 and the last boat travelled the Pontypridd to Cardiff section in 1942.

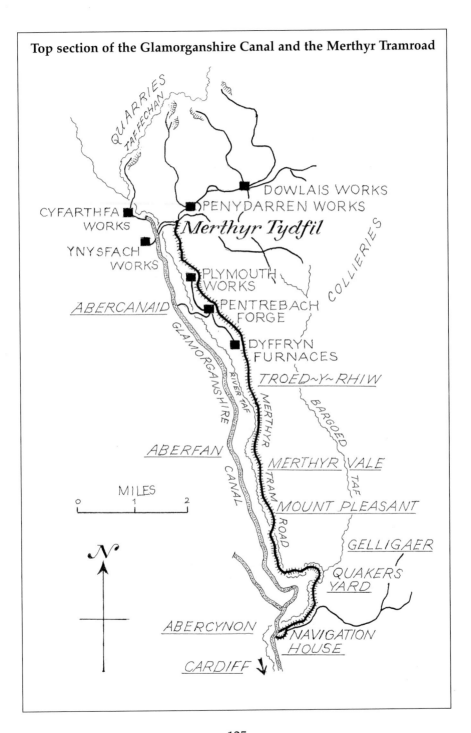

Top section of the Glamorganshire Canal and the Merthyr Tramroad

QUARRIES

TAF FECHAN

DOWLAIS WORKS

PENYDARREN WORKS

CYFARTHFA WORKS

Merthyr Tydfil

YNYSFACH WORKS

COLLIERIES

PLYMOUTH WORKS

ABERCANAID

PENTREBACH FORGE

DYFFRYN FURNACES

TROED~Y~RHIW

GLAMORGANSHIRE

RIVER TAF

MERTHYR TRAM ROAD

BARGOED

TAF

ABERFAN

MERTHYR VALE

MILES

0   1   2

CANAL

MOUNT PLEASANT

GELLIGAER

N

QUAKERS YARD

ABERCYNON

NAVIGATION HOUSE

CARDIFF ↓

Cyfartha Ironworks was once the largest in the world

It was only the Cyfarthfa Ironworks that was directly served by the Glamorganshire Canal. This works had its beginnings in 1765 when Anthony Hill opened a small charcoal-burning furnace just below the confluence of the Taff Fawr and the Taff Fechan. Richard Crawshay, a Yorkshireman, leased the workings in 1786 and bought them in 1794. By the beginning of the nineteenth century, four blast furnaces complete with charging and cast houses, had been built against a natural bank on the western side of the Taff Valley. In 1815 the works had seven furnaces in operation, producing 18,000 tons of iron a year and by 1849 this figure had risen to 166,800 tons. The works then employed about 5,000 people, of whom 190 were women. Between the 1790s and 1830, Cyfarthfa was the world's largest and most profitable ironworks before being overtaken by neighbouring Dowlais Works. In the 1880s the original furnaces were replaced with more modern ones, built for a steelworks and in 1902 the works were sold to Guest, Keen and Nettlefold (GKN) who closed it in 1910.

At Cyfarthfa, today, can be seen some of the best surviving 19th century furnace structures in the world. Beneath the old furnaces are labyrinths of blast passages which helped raise internal temperatures to 1,500 degrees Celsius.

Mostyn Evan decides to relocate to the Vale of Neath

On seeing *"a new-fangled Trevethick engine, fussing up and down pulling"*, Mostyn comments *"It sings a song of death for the barges.... We can see which way the wind is blowing. Ten years from now the barges in this valley will begin to fail."*

Soon afterwards, Mostyn decides to move his family to the Vale of Neath, where the railway had not yet arrived and the *'canal is still alive and kicking.'* The Bargee Union in that valley would not allow them to buy a barge on the Neath Canal, so Mostyn decides that the only way to get around the Union regulations is to buy a barge in the Taff Valley, haul it down the canal to Cardiff and then sail it out into the open sea to Baglan Bay and then up the Neath Canal from Briton Ferry.

A half-finished barge is duly purchased from Eli Cohen, a barge builder in Abercynon. Three months later it is completed and ready for the epic journey to Resolven in the Vale of Neath.

Loaded up with all their possessions, including a mule and a donkey, the Evan family take the barge down to Cardiff and enter the sea-pound that leads into the Bristol Channel. They raise a mast and sail and, rounding Penarth Head, they sail up the coast to reach:

> *"... the mouth of the Neath river, poled and towed past Giant's Grave and up to Neath Abbey, which was smoking and flaring her ironworks like a place demented, and out came the puddlers and rollers and scarecrow Irish, all waving and cheering us, for it is not every day of the week that a twenty-two ton coal loader runs up to Red Jacket with a sail in tatters, its crew at the oars, a mule and a donkey aboard and fowls in the rigging..."*

When they reach the Aqueduct at Aberdulais, a woman comes out of Lock Cottage with her adopted daughter Rhiannon, to work the paddles. She is Mari Mortymer who appeared in the previous two books. With the other members of the Mortymer family now either dead or dispersed, she has left Cae White in Carmarthenshire and settled in the Neath Valley, where she has obtained employment as a lock keeper. For Mostyn it is love at first sight.

> *"The lock at Aberdulais appeared deserted when we arrived, and only when I began to swing the paddle did the door open and the keeper come out: pale and proud, she looked, smiling with cool politeness as my father bowed."*

The Evan family then travel on to Resolven and reach their destination, the *"Old Navigation, a tumbledown, ragged three-storey canal inn, used by the early bargees and drovers, with a rusted creaking sign twenty feet up to prove it."*

Neath Canal at Rheola

The Vale of Neath

I remember discussing *Song of the Earth* with Alex back in 1986 and he told me that when he was researching material for the novel, he spent many enjoyable weekends exploring the Vale of Neath and talking to the local people. It was not long before he decided that he needed a temporary base, to avoid the need to travel back and forth from Abergavenny each day. He towed his caravan to Resolven, and initially parked it on the side of the canal. When he was requested to move it, someone suggested that he should ask Mr Hull at Crugau Farm near Rheola if he could put it in on his land.

It was always a joy to go there after a week at work, doing his job as a Quantity Surveyor and Alex told me that the time spent researching this novel was one of his fondest memories.

Alexander Cordell parked his caravan at Crugau Farm for use as a weekend base whilst researching *Song of the Earth*

Evenings were spent in the Vale of Neath pubs, chatting to local characters over pints of ale. He also spent time sitting on park benches, listening to the old miners and retired railwaymen, who always had fascinating stories to tell. It was undoubtedly their valuable contributions that enabled Alex to bring his novel to life, providing such a vivid portrayal of life in the Neath Valley as it would have been in the mid nineteenth century.

He once emphasised to me that the facts in his novels were all based on careful research, "into local history, public records, births, deaths and marriage certificates, company records - in fact anything which relates to the period of which I am writing. "

* * * * * * * * * * * * *

From my home at Llanfoist, near Abergavenny, it only takes me about forty minutes to drive along the A465 to reach the Neath Valley. This beautiful valley, running between two ridges, was ground out by a glacier during the Ice Ages. The valley floor is on average about half-a-mile wide, and the sides are steep, in fact very steep in places. To the east is Craig-y-Llyn which rises to nearly 2,000 feet and on the western side is Hir Fynydd (The Long Mountain). This rises to 1,600 feet and carries the Roman trackway known as Sarn Helen.

The valley sides are well wooded, but in the 19th century the slopes would have been comparatively bare, for the trees were felled for fuel. Replanting was begun by the Forestry Commission in 1922,when Rheola Forest, covering some 8,000 acres was planted with conifers.

Along the valley floor, the river Nedd winds it way down, dropping just 250 feet in the whole course from Pontneddfechan to the sea.

On arriving in **Glyn Neath**, I stopped to look for the terminus of the Neath Canal, but unfortunately the old basin at Maes Marchog, which would have been in the vicinity of Oddfellows Street on the south east side of the A465 has long been destroyed.

The canal head was also the terminus of Tappenden's Tramroad, which for a short time linked the Neath Canal with the Aberdare Canal. There is a stone bridge crossing the river Cynon at SN 990243 which carried this tramroad, and it has the date 1834 on its keystone. Tramroads also ran from the canal head to Pont Nedd Fechan and the Dinas Silica Mines.

Glyn Neath would have been a hive of industry in those times, with horse stables, warehouses and powder stores, providing employment for a large number of people. There would have also been several pubs here and one of interest is the *Lamb and Flag,* situated in Wellfield Place, but it is not the original building.

The *Lamb and Flag* Inn at Glyn Neath

Rheola House was the home of the Vaughan family

Nearby **Pont Walby**, where "Man Arfon Agent" had his base and it was there that Mostyn obtained a contract for hauling coal from Glyn Neath to Giant's Grave, making three trips a week.

A brickworks was established at Pont Walby in the 1820s by William Weston Young, who developed a method of producing high quality fire bricks. Silica mined at Pont Nedd Fechan was ground and moulded into bricks which were then cured in kilns. The Dinas firebricks were exported all over Europe and America to be used in lining the blast furnaces of iron and steelworks. Pontwalby brickworks closed in 1920.

I now continued along the old main road, stopping shortly to examine a cast-iron aqueduct, which was built to carry a fast flowing stream over the canal and into the adjoining river Neath. It bears the inscription 'NEATH ABBEY IRONWORKS GLAMORGANSHIRE 1835'.

Cast iron aqueduct carrying a stream over the Neath Canal

Soon, I was passing through **Rheola**, a name which comes from Hirolau (long trackway). Heol is Welsh for road and the name has become confused. Situated in parkland above the road is the rather grand Rheola House which was originally a farmhouse. It was purchased in 1800 by John Edwards, a London lawyer, who was related to the famous regency architect John Nash. In 1815, Edwards persuaded his clever relation to come here and redesign the house that he had acquired.

Restored lock at Rheola

In order to gain a legacy, John Edwards changed his surname to Vaughan. When he died in 1833, he left a large portion of his estate to John Edward Vaughan's son who was named Nash Vaughan Edwards Vaughan. It was certainly a complicated matter!

At one time the house was used as a Residential Training Centre, owned by the British Aluminium Company, but today it is in private ownership. Cordell mentions the Rheola Vaughans living here:

> *"There was a ball at Vaughan Rheola last Friday night. Passing on the road between the lodges, I did see them, sitting on the lawns after the dancing."*

> *"Often, especially on Sunday nights the Vaughans of Rheola would come up from Aberdulais aqueduct in barges with choirs, and beautiful it was to hear the full harmony of the ancient hymns, and always they sang in Welsh."*

Resolven Basin

On reaching **Resolven** I left my car in a public car park near the canal Basin. From there it is just a short walk along the towpath in the Glyn Neath direction to reach a small building called Ty Banc. This 18th century lengthman's cottage provided inspiration for Cordell, to form the basis of his Old Navigation Inn.

Ty Banc, an 18th century lengthsman's cottage was used by Cordell as the basis for the Old Navigation Inn. It is now a Tea and Gift Shop, open in the summer to visitors.

Interior of Ty Banc Tea Shop

Ty Banc has been restored in recent years and turned into a Tea and Gift Shop, which is open in the summer and run by the Glamorgan Association for the Disabled.

Significantly the cottage was last occupied by Mr and Mrs Will Evans, who would have been living there at the time when Alex was carrying out his research. It would seem that he dropped the 's' when he made Mostyn Evan one of his main characters in the book. Wil Evans was known as Wil Banc and after his time the cottage became deserted and quickly fell into ruins until it was restored in recent years.

Some years previously, I had visited Resolven to see Grantley and Gwynneth Davis, who had got to know Alex very well when he was researching background material for *Song of the Earth*. At that time they kept a newsagents, which was the oldest shop in the village. It had previously been owned by Grantley's father, who was the local gents' haidresser. The shop finally closed in 1996, after being in existence for nearly a century.

When *Song of the Earth* was published, Alex persuaded Mr and Mrs Davis to sell copies at their shop on a sale or return basis. The hardback version was priced at 30 shillings and they sold about 200 copies to local people.

Whilst Alex had many happy memories of time spent in Resolven, it was also the place where Rosina, his first wife died. This tragic event occurred on a day in March 1972, when he was giving a talk in Pontrydyfen. Rosina had not been feeling well, so it was decided that she should spend the afternoon with Mr and Mrs Morris, another couple who lived in the village and had become friends. While Alex was away giving his lecture, Rosina had a heart attack and passed away. They had married in 1937 and the day of her death was their 35th wedding anniversary.

It was Mr Morris who had shown Alex some of the interesting places in the valley and he had a good knowledge of local history. Sadly, he died soon afterwards as well.

I then returned to the old main road and followed it down to **Aberdulais** which is a very interesting location. First of all, I paid a visit to Aberdulais Falls Visitor Center which is owned and run by the National Trust.

The story of this site spans over 400 years, starting with the first manufacture of copper in 1584, when a smelting works was established here by Ulrich Frosse on behalf of the Mines Royal Company and by 1667 an iron forge was operating here as well as a corn mill. A tin-plate works was built around 1830 and also a grist mill.

The industrial remains at Aberdulais belong to a tin plate works that opened in 1830 and closed about 1890

Aberdulais Falls

Neath Borough Council made a gift of this historic site to the National Trust in 1981. The Trust built a Hydro Electric scheme here in 1991 and the Waterwheel is the biggest in Europe which generates electricity. The site is open from April to December.

Leaving the National Trust site, I crossed the road to pass under the bridge beside the river Neath (Afon Nedd). There are some very impressive stone structures here including the 340ft long Aberdulais aqueduct and the later viaduct which carried the railway. At the end of the aqueduct can be seen a lock and the keeper's cottage where Cordell installed Mari Mortymer and her adopted daughter Rhiannon.

I walked on past the Railway Tavern and then beneath the old railway bridge to reach Aberdulais Canal Basin, which is situated at the junction of the Neath and Tennant Canals.

This 340ft long aqueduct spanning the river Neath at Aberdulais was completed by William Kirkhouse in 1824. Ten masonry arches span the river and there is a small tollhouse at the Neath end of the aqueduct.

The **Neath Canal** was built under an Act of 1791, from Glyn Neath down the valley of the Neath river to Melincrythan Pill, below Neath. Its purpose was to enable iron ore to be transported from the upper part of the Vale of Neath to the ironworks situated at Cwm Gwrach, Melin-y-Cwrt, Penrhiwtyn, Aberdulais and Neath Abbey. Also, it provided a means of transporting coal from the valley collieries to the coast for export to many parts of the world.

Thomas Dadford Junior was the engineer in charge of building the lower section and work began in 1791 at Brick Field, near Melyn Crythan Pill. After twelve months the work was taken over byThomas Sheasby, but he left the scene in 1794 and the canal was completed the following year by direct labour.

Four years later it was extended from Melincrythan to Giant's Grave, near Briton Ferry. This section incorporated a private canal known as the Penrhiwtyn, which had been built some years earlier by Lord Vernon from Giant's Grave to Penrhiwtyn. In a document of 1795 it was described as being in length 1 mile 592 yards from its end to Giant's Grave Pill. On a plan (c.1795) of the Penrhiwtyn furnaces, this canal is shown with a small dock for unloading on the line of the railway at Herbert Road. The stretch of the canal between the bridge at this point and that near the 'Chemical Pill', was apparently made to join up the existing canals.

The total length of the Neath Canal was 10.5 miles and it had 19 locks, which could take boats about 60 feet long by 9 feet beam, carrying 25 tons. The cargoes were coal, iron ore, limestone, silica and gunpowder. Coal was the most lucrative cargo and during the late 1850's, 20,000 tons annually were being transported on the canal.

In 1866 the traders were complaining that the Neath canal 'had gradually become so neglected that it was half filled with mud and allowed such an escape or waste of water as to render it impossible for the navigation of barges carrying more than half their ordinary load of 24 tons each.'

By 1880 all the coal was being carried on the Vale of Neath railway and the canal trade died. The last commercial boat on the canal ran in 1916 and navigation on the canal finally ceased in 1934.

Restoration work has been undertaken by the Neath and Tennant Preservation Society. This society was formed in 1974 with the aim of restoring navigation on the entire length of the canal.

'I believe railways are better than canals and will supersede them.'

William Crawshay of Cyfarthfa, 1832

Locks on the Neath Canal (Neath - Maesmarchog)

1. Lock House
2. Lock Machine
3. Witworth Lock
4. Gitto Lock
5. Ynysarwed Lock
6. Abergarwed Lock
7. Farmer's Lock
8. Resolven Lock
9. Crugiau Lock
10. Rheola Lock
11. Aber-clwyd Lock
12. Ynisultor Lock
13. Maes-gwyn Lock
14. Bwllfa's Lock
15. Granery Lock
16. Chain Lock
17. Foxe's Lock
18. Lamb Lock
19. Maesmarchog Lock

The **Tennant Canal** was started in 1821 by George Tennant of Cadoxton, with William Kirkhouse as his engineer, to provide an extension to the Glan-y-wern and Red Jacket Canals. It opened on May 14th 1824, when ten barges of coal were conveyed from the Vale of Neath to the shipping place at Swansea. This waterway carried a great deal of trade up until the 1890s when the Vale of Neath Railway started taking most of its business. The last commercial traffic on this canal was in 1934.

It is remarkable that on the 8.5 miles, from Aberdulais to Swansea, there is not a single lock on this canal. But the junction with the Neath Canal at Aberdulais required a 'stupendous and magnificent ten-arched aqueduct which took a year to build. George Tennant also built a dock at the seaward end of the canal.

"I hear again the run of the Nedd, smell again
the sweet sour earth smell of the cut: aye all
the song of the earth is with me."

The Tennant Canal passes in front of the monastic buildings of Neath Abbey. Nearby was a short private branch canal to the ironworks.

Neath Abbey was founded in 1111 by Richard de Granville of Bideford and the architect was a man called Lalys, who also designed Margam Abbey. In 1542 the abbey was dissolved and sold to Sir Richard Cromwell for £731. He subsequently sold it to Sir Thomas Stradling and Christopher Turberville. In the 17th century, the Abbot's House was converted into a sizeable mansion by the Herberts of Swansea. The ruins of Neath Abbey are now in the care of Cadw, Welsh Historic Monuments, and open to the public.

The Neath Abbey Ironworks (SS 738977) was founded in 1792 by George Fox and his brothers, together with Peter Price. They had come from Falmouth in Cornwall, where there was a Quaker colony. Its purpose was at first to produce pig iron and castings.

The Rev Richard Warner, an 18th century travel writer, who visited the works soon after they opened, commented that he had seen "two immense blast furnaces constantly at work. They are blown by iron bellows worked by a double engine with a steam cylinder of 40 inches in diameter. A foundry also attracted our attention."

One of the two large blast furnaces of the Neath Abbey Ironworks, which was begun in 1795, have survived and also the original workshops. The Neath Abbey Iron Co. became famous for the manufacture of all kinds of machinery, pumps, boilers, stationary engines and locomotives. In 1841 the works employed 213 people including 175 adults, 47 under the age of 18 and 11 under 13 years. The Quaker ownership of the ironworks ended in 1874 when the works finally closed.

In 1798 the Neath Abbey Iron Co. was making pig-iron, using ironstone carried down the Neath Canal from Aberpergwm. A short private branch of the canal led to the works.

By the early 19th century, the works were run by Joseph Tregalles Price who had strong beliefs and refused to manufacture cannon during the Napoleonic wars despite the fact that they were in much demand. A few other ironmasters followed his example.

In about 1830 the works began to supply locomotives and by 1832 they were building them for the Dowlais Ironworks. The first one was the 'Perseverance' which cost £630. The works continued to develop and by the middle of the 19th century it had become an important centre for ironmaking, engineering and shipbuilding.

George Borrow visited Neath abbey in 1854 and in his book *Wild Wales* he describes the ruins as being among "grimy, diabolical-looking buildings, huge heaps of cinders and black rubbish, a pool as black as soot in a swamp of disgusting leaden colour."

John Murray who wrote a *Handbook to South Wales* in 1870, was also disappointed with the place for he found the abbey, "defaced by the smoke and coal-dust of the neighbouring extensive copper and ironworks. Though now so unsightly and contaminated with black stains, it was originally a structure of great extent and magnificence."

The ironworks passed through various hands of the Fox-Price family but, eventually, in 1874, the Quaker partnership ceased and the works closed down. Two of the blast furnaces have survived and a plaque on the wall of a house near the entrance to the site reads:

'Tregelles Price lived at this house. He was the founder of the Peace Society, the oldest in the world. He was not disobedient to the heavenly vision.'

Tregelles Price was the eldest son of Peter and Anna Tregelles Price, who belonged to the Quaker Industrialist contingent who left Cornwall for Neath at the end of the 19th century. There is no doubt that he was the mastermind behind the wide range of industrial activities at Neath Abbey Works. He died on Christmas Day 1854, and was buried in the Friends Meeting House graveyard in Neath.

Near the end of the Neath Canal at Giant's Grave

It was the enterprising George Tennant, owner of the Cadoxton estate, who linked the Red Jacket tidal creek with the Tawe and Neath rivers by widening and extending it and building a lock at each end. In addition he constructed a branch canal 1.5 miles long to Glan-y-wern.

By 1824 he had linked his canal (the Tennant Canal) with the Neath Canal at Aberdulais to achieve a complete route from Glyn Neath all the way to Swansea Docks. At the Swansea end, he bought wharves on a tidal inlet of the Tawe and his canal terminal became known as Port Tennant, before it became known as Swansea.

In 1827 a passenger service was introduced on the Tennant Canal from Neath to Port Tennant, providing a slow journey by horse-drawn barge and this was in operation until the railway opened in 1850.

The Red Jacket Pill was later made deeper and wider to enable larger vessels to pass through and it continued to be used until 1926.

At **Tonna** can be seen the last of the 19 locks on the Neath Canal, a lock keeper's cottage and the canal company stables. In 1934 the last traditional wooden canal boat to be constructed in Wales was built in the workshop here by Ben Jones, Foreman of the Neath Canal Co. It was named *Ivy May* after his wife.

It is at Tonna that Isambard Kingdom Brunel appears in the novel:

> *"With an expressionless face the man on the bank watched the scene below him, and his navvies moved nervously, like schoolboys caught at a prank. This was the engineer they loved, the man of genius who was building bridges and viaducts, aqueducts and tunnels, and driving railways all over Britain."*

Brunel had been told by his rival Stephenson that he considered it "impossible to make a line adapted to the transport of minerals and that the difficulties were insurmountable".

However, Brunel was a man who enjoyed a challenge. He built a 1 in 50 gradient from Glyn Neath to Hirwaun and a fine viaduct at Cwm Gwrelych, consisting of four bays each of 43 feet span and 60 feet high. A tunnel was built at Pencaedrain and wooden bridges had to be constructed over the river and canal at Neath and Aberdulais. The line was laid on the broad gauge (7ft) and stations were built at Neath, Aberdulais, Resolven, Glynneath, Hirwaun and Abernant.

> *"Brunel , the genius had done what Stephenson said could not be done - linked the wealth of the towns of Aberdare and Neath, and collecting the vast tonnage of Merthyr Road, Hirwaun, Glyn Neath, Resolven and Aberdulais had poured it into the maws of the sea."*

Isambard Kingdom Brunel (1806-59) was the greatest engineer of the Industrial Revolution. He had been educated in Britain and France and set up as a civil engineer in 1830. At the age of 27, in 1833, he was appointed engineer to the Bristol to London Railway, later known as the Great Western Railway.

The thought of a railway coming through the Vale of Neath was most disturbing for the local farming community. Siân Glover, who lived in a cottage at Pont Walby, expressed concern that the heavy puff of the engine would sour the contents of the milk pails, all the way along the route of the line. Likewise, the landlord of the *Plough Inn* at Abertwrch was concerned that the smoke of the locomotives passing so close to his home would kill the horses in his stables.

At Tonna can be seen the last of the nineteen locks on the Neath Canal and a lock keeper's cottage

Early 18th century workshops at Tonna, where in 1934 the Neath Canal Co. built their last traditional wooden narrow boat, which was called the *Ivy May*.

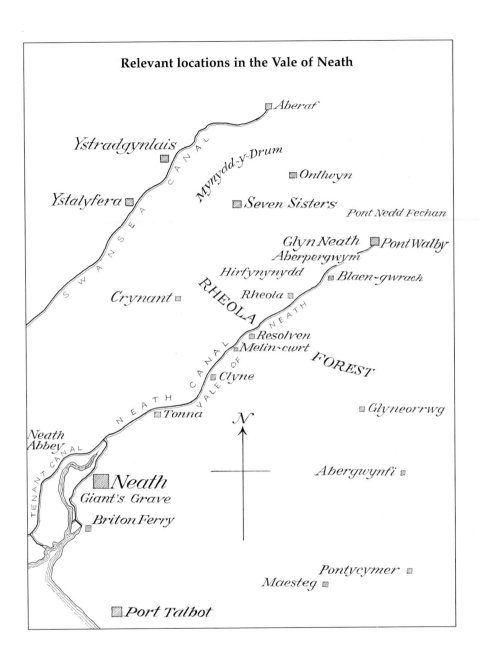

Relevant locations in the Vale of Neath

Restored locks at Clyne

A few miles beyond Clyne is the village of Melincourt which is well known for its beautiful waterfall.

Use was made of the river to turn a water wheel, which worked the bellows of an early ironworks established by John Hanbury of Pontypool. The water wheel was described by Richard Warner when he came here in 1798. He said that its circumference was 120 feet which would accordingly give a diameter of about 38 feet and he mentioned that the works consisted of 'a blast furnace, a finery and a foundry.' The illustration shows a channel carrying water to a wheel which worked the furnace bellows. The furnace was powered by charcoal made from timber obtained from Vale of Neath.

This 75 feet waterfall is also called Rhyd-yr-Hesg and the famous artist J.M.W. Turner came here in 1795 to produce a drawing which is now in the British Museum. He also did a painting of the waterfall at Aberdulais.

The Family move to Resolven

"Getting into the Old Navigation that June was like trying to enter a besieged town, with the main line on one side of it, the Rheola branch line on the other and its back garden specially selected by Man Arfon for a rail and sleeper stocking compound."

"The Old Navigation was dying on her feet, and we knew it. And we were dying, too. ... the barge hauls came less and less, as colliery after colliery built access tram-roads or blasted deep into the rock for cuttings and platforms, our savings dwindled to nothing. Also, since Dewi, Ifor and me were working part time in Resolven Colliery now, my father could not take a barge haul even when it was offered."

Mostyn decided that the time had come to leave the *Old Navigation* and move to a terraced cottage in Resolven and go back to working in coal which was his original form of employment.

"The sun was high when we trundled the hearse away up past Crugau and along the road to the Biben Inn and took left over the river and into Resolven. Past the canal loading bay we went and along by New Inn, with men raising hats at the hearse and women dropping curtseys; up past the Square to Lyons Row, and down to Number sixteen where our women were waiting... A new life: a new village with a name that stood square to the world, its chin hazed with the blue of manhood, with hair on its chest and a hook in either hand. Resolven."

Bryn tells us that:

"Athough I loved the Old Navigation I loved this Big Street in Resolven better ... for it is good to have people living closer about you with their smells of cooking in your kitchen and their warmth and sounds coming into your heart. And houses joined together in rows I do like especially, since they are like a gang of colliers going out on a razzle, arms linked in warmth..."

"Lovely, it is to live in a street, I say with all the excitement of the men coming home and the women sitting outside their backs and handing out all the cheek in the world. Smoke from the chimneys stood as straight as bars and the air was perfumed with the scent of burning pine, and the mist was falling with September over the vale."

Cottages in Lyons Place, Resolven, but unfortunately number 16, where the Evan family would have resided has been demolished

Zion Methodist Chapel in Resolven was built in 1838, rebuilt in 1869 and turned into a Community Centre in 1999. It was here that Mostyn Evan married Mari Mortymer.

"And so, in summer, my father took the woman Mari Mortymer to Resolven Zion and brought her out as wife."

Aberdare and the Cynon Valley

Mostyn's eldest son Ifor is killed in an accident at Resolven Colliery and for the sake of his widow Rebecca, the family decide to move from the Vale of Neath and travel to Aberdare on the new railway.

Returning up the A465, I drove past Glynneath and ascended the long hill to **Hirwaun**, which just like Blaenavon, is a town that developed around its ironworks. Established in 1757, this was the first coke-smelting furnace to be established in South Wales and by 1819 it was in the ownership of Francis Crawshay.

This eccentric ironmaster, a son of the 'Iron King', William Crawshay (1788-1867), was the only member of his family to learn Welsh. He was very popular with his workers and it is said that nothing pleased them more than to hear him swear at them in their own tongue!

Francis Crawshay is also remembered for having constructed a stone tower known as 'Crawshay's Folly', on the mountainside to the west of Hirwaun.

Completely circular it originally stood thirty feet high. Its inside measurement was twelve feet in diameter, and the outer circumference fifty-eight feet. It was a three-storied building, with a room on each floor. The roof was made of iron and in addition to the six arched windows there were six round holes in the tower wall in three pairs facing north, east and

Crawshay's Folly

west respectively. These were presumably intended for shooting through in the event of an attack. Francis Crawshay lived here during the summer months and his weapons included two brass cannons.

Tower Colliery, near Hirwaun, takes its name from Crawshay's Folly and following the employees' successful buy-out is the last deep mine to operate in Wales.

From Hirwaun, I followed the A4059 to **Aberdare** which is situated at the confluence of the rivers Cynon and Dare. The Cynon is the larger of the two and it rises at Llygad y Cynon (Eye of the Cynon), just north of Hirwaun, and flows down to join the Taff at Abercynon.

Before industry arrived, the Cynon Valley was a rural area of small villages, isolated farms and remote uplands. Population in the valley began to increase when the first ironworks was opened at Llwydcoed, near Aberdare. This was followed by the Abernant Ironworks two years later and the Gadlys Ironworks in 1827. Ironworking ceased in 1875, when there was a great strike in Glamorgan, and the Cynon Valley thereafter depended mostly upon the coal trade for its wealth.

The first colliery at Aberdare was opened in 1840, by Thomas Powell, a timber merchant from Newport and by the end of the nineteenth century there were numerous pits producing about two million tons of coal a year.

To improve my knowledge of the history of this locality, I first made my way to the Cynon Valley Museum, which is well signposted and housed in a former tramshed of the old Gadlys Ironworks (SO 001030) which ceased production in 1866. The surviving buildings include two blast furnaces, a blowing-engine house, casting house and workshops.

Today, Aberdare is a very pleasant town with good shops and facilities, but in the 1850's it was a very different matter.

> *"You have to see this Aberdare to believe it. I thought I had seen some places up in Merthyr, but Bute Street and Wigan Row where the north country English lived was as bad as anything I had seen up The Top, and Hirwaun and Club Row were not fit for pigs - and all owned by Lord Bute."*

> *"Acres of the bright, clay soil were ponds of human filth: the cesspits, where they existed, had overflowed and in some houses at Cobblers Row, near the vicarage, the night-soil in the ground floor rooms was inches deep."*

> *"In the gutters sat beggars, men and women who were the burnedout slag of the ironworks, the refuse of profit that was shovelled away by the likes of Wayne of Gadlys and Bailey of Aberaman, and all to no end, for his works, built ten years back, was never a success."*

The Cynon Valley Museum is housed in part of the old Gadlys Ironworks

I made my way to Library Square which stands in an area once known as Green Fach. The old houses have been demolished but it was Number Five, where Cordell placed Mostyn and his family.

> *"They told us that Number Five, Green Fach had only been up twenty years but it looked more like two hundred with its stained walls and the piles of refuse at the front and back, with no garden save a pond of stinking cess-pit overflow along its unpaved street, and no light came into the rooms save red flickerings from the distant ironworks, and there was nowhere big enough to swing a cat."*

> *"If you have seen Green Fach in the'fifties up in Aberdare: if you have smelled Green Fach as we smelled it that summer dusk, you would have known something worse than the slums of Asia, said my father."*

They begin work at the Lletty Shankins mine, but it is not long before they are caught up in a two month strike to resist a reduction in wages.

> *"Come the end of that June the whole of the Aberdare Valley between Hirwaun and Mountain Ash was out on strike. Short of coal for their fires, the ironworks began to blow out their furnaces, beginning with the Gadlys up to the big Abernant. Five thousand colliers in pits big and small, in drift and level and mine, struck in the valley against the fifteen per cent reduction in their wages."*

> *"In July, from Aberdare to Abercynon, the children, always the first, began to die, and the little yellow coffins went trailing up the hillsides: the sick and aged began to follow, then the vagrants. They died in scores from the small-pox; of typhoid and cholera. They died in the sink-pits of Wigan Row, Hirwaun Row and Club Row, and Bute Street, which is named after the landlord of undernourishment and the lack of good water."*

> *"At the hands of coal and ironmasters who couldn't afford to lay a decent water supply in a land abundant with water, or lay a decent drain in a land of slope and incline; this is how they died."*

After suffering much hardship the Evan family decide to break the strike rather than starve to death, and with military protection they make their way to the Gadlys Pit.

Milestone erected by the Health Board

This small church of St John, of simple design, is believed to have been built in 1189. Outside its west door are the original iron gates made at the Abernant Works, consisting of a series of the figure 3 (ninety-six in all). In the churchyard is the grave of David Williams of Aberaman, who in 1789 insisted on being buried standing upright, to be ready at the Day of Judgement.

The Bute Arms, Aberdare

"And so, on the fiftieth day of the strike we stood in the Row of Green Fach and awaited the coming of the protection military... Down Unity Street and Ty Fry the strikers were lining the road three deep, racing up from Cannon and Commercial and Bute, buttoning up and belting up and smoothing straight from their beds. And in the red tinged light of dawn they lent their bawled insults to the workers of Gadlys, forming an avenue down which we walked. Here were soldiers in scores, sabres drawn, their horses plunging among the tattered buildings of the ironworks of Wayne..."

"On, on we went along the avenue of hatred and threats, their fists an inch from our faces as the soldiers fought to keep them back. Enveloped by their fury and insults we went... the howling reached a new thunder as we neared the shaft of Gadlys..."

I walked through Aberdare following the route that the Evan family would have taken from their little cottage in Green Fach to reach the Gadlys Pit. It has of course been swept away and now merely gives its name to a car park.

"A swine was this Wayne Gadlys: she began in the drop beside St John's and ran in a mile drift to Fothergill, the beating heart of Abernant and the mushrooming scarlet of the furnaces of Forge Side. And the workers of Colliers' Row and Engineers' Row knew Gadlys for the bitch she was."

"And if the bell-stone and dram and hoof and engine don't get you down Gadlys, the chances are that water would, for she was loaded to the gunwales in underwater ponds and streams and old, flooded workings."

They worked in the Gadlys Pit for three days and had to face the angry mob each time. Cordell, now leads us into a sad climax to his stirring novel, with the lives of Mostyn and Mari coming to an abrupt end. Bryn gives a heart rending account of how he tries to save his father and stepmother:

> *"With death threatening I did not recognise it: it seemed impossible, with the gallery but feet away, that anybody would die, least of all my father, who was indestructible; or Mari, who was in his care. Taking a deep breath against the roof, I ducked under the water again and crawled round the pillar into Four Stall once more, taking the middle this time, hands sweeping out for a hold. Something brushed my searching hand and I plunged deeper into the blackness. Here a fresh surge of colder water enveloped me from the old workings and I swayed towards it, feeling the rock face, trying desperately to keep direction. And suddenly Mari's dress streamed over me, caressing my face, my naked chest. Gripping it, I pushed backwards, falling to my right, and I struck the coal pillar. Up now, into air, gasping and retching. With one hand gripping the dress and the other pulling me round the pillar, I collected into Two Stall, and ducked under the flood again, dragging Mari upright against me, lifting her face into air."*

> *"I do not know how long I sat there with Mari in my arms, now in pitch blackness, for the last lamp had gone out. And although the flood had not risen higher than my chest, there was a great pressure in my ears and it was difficult to breathe."*

> *"I knew that my father was dead, for the next stall, being lower on the drift, would have filled to the roof. In darkness I lowered my face against Mari's and wept."*

"I wept when in *Song of the Earth,* Mari died in Bryn's arms in the flooded mine. It's unprofessional I know, but that's my chemistry."

Alexander Cordell

The novel closes with Bryn returning to the *Old Navigation*, where he re-lives memories of happy times there before the railway changed everything. He had come back, because he felt complete in this place which he had once loved so much, but standing in the garden he suddenly realised that *"it was the law of life itself that change must come about; it was the law of God that life went on."*

"And I saw before me not a land of defeat and exploitation, but a land of triumph. I saw in the scarred landscape and the tunneled mountains not a desecration but the glory of their wealth."

"It was as if I myself had been re-born, that the spirit of my country had moved in me, making me one with her in all her stubborn courage."

Bryn then makes his way to Crugau and scrambles aboard the low-loader of a passing train which was just gathering speed.

"Lying there gasping, staring at the astonishing blue of the sky with the clatter of the rails thumping through my shoulders as we gathered speed. And in the very power of the new inventions the joy in me grew, filling me with an exhuberance I had never known before. I scrambled up, splaying my legs to the swaying flat with the wind whistling through my hair and flattening my clothes. The Corsair belched smoke, flying soot struck my face in needles of pain, but I rejoiced in the action and movement and strength of it all. Over Pencydrain viaduct we went, rattling, bucking, with a hundred-foot drop into the valley below, and over my shoulder I saw the flowing land of the Vale of Neath in all its summer beauty. Resolven Mountain I saw, and the wooded slopes of the Forest of Rheola, and in the heart of it the old Nedd was leaping down to the sea and the canal cut a staggering needle of silver through the summer gold and green down to Aberdulais. The beauty of it caught my breath, and I could have shouted with the joy of it."

ALEXANDER CORDELL

THIS PROUD AND SAVAGE LAND

The Prelude to 'Rape of the Fair Country'

THIS PROUD AND SAVAGE LAND

"Aye, what is there in a town that enmeshes the soul? One thing was certain; this town was worth fighting for, dying for if needs be; no not the sagging walls but the people within those walls. I smiled at her roofs and chimneys outlined against the summer moon. I looked once more at Blaenafon."

A few weeks after the publication of my book *Cordell Country*, Alex and his wife Donnie invited me to spend a long weekend with them at their home on the Isle of Man. It was my first visit to the island and my hosts took great delight in taking me on a tour of some of their favourite places.

In a pub one evening, whilst enjoying a pint of beer, I began to talk about a possible theme for a book that could be Alex's next novel. The idea that I put to him was that he should write a novel telling the story of Hywel Mortymer leading up to the time when his son Iestyn was born, thus providing a prelude to his most famous novel, *Rape of the Fair Country*.

Alex was very enthusiastic about my suggestion and within a week he had completed a draft synopsis and obtained a commission from his publisher to write the novel. During the next twelve months he made regular visits to Abergavenny and we undertook numerous research trips, visiting locations which might be included in the plot.

In 1800, Hywel Mortymer, aged sixteen, suddenly orphaned and penniless, makes his way from his birthplace in Mid Wales to seek work in the mines and ironworks of Blaenavon. An important theme of the book is the exploitation of child labour and Cordell set out to portray the grim working conditions that young people were employed under during those turbulent times.

The novel is also packed with many of the characters which we also meet later in *Rape of the Fair Country*. For example there is the unforgettable Iolo Milk, Big Rhys Jenkins, Tomos Traherne the preacher and of course the Mortymers themselves - Hywel, Elianor, Morfydd, Edwina and Iestyn who comes into the story at the end of the book.

It was fascinating to work with Alexander Cordell and to help him with his research by providing historical information. I also introduced him to several of the locations which appear in the book; such as the Gold Mines at Pumpsaint, the Devil's Bridge in the Clydach Gorge, the site of Capel Newydd near Blaenafon and the *Goose and Cuckoo Inn* above Llanover.

Loyal readers of Cordell's works will surely agree that no other writer has ever managed to capture the atmosphere and spirit of 19th century Wales so well.

In this novel he set out to provide convincing evidence of the exploitation of child labour in the mines and ironworks of nineteenth-century Britain, for it was his opinion that little had been written on this matter by modern historians.

Thousands of young children would have been seen in the villages around the ironworks. Crawshay of Merthyr employed more than four hundred children, fifty of these being girls, while Hill of the Merthyr Plymouth Ironworks employed, apart from a thousand men, a hundred and fifty boys and girls.

Evidence of this can be seen in the Commissioners' Reports (The Blue Books) of 1847 and the Commission of Enquiry into the State of Children in Employment (1840s). These are held at the National Archives, Public Records Office, Richmond Surrey.

Life for children working in iron is encapsulated by a statement made by William Lloyd, the furnaces manager of Blaenafon Ironworks, who said:

"I have about 37 children working about the furnaces under my charge, the youngest being about seven years old. I have some boys between eight and twelve years old helping the 'fillers' at the furnace top (tipping in the fuel and ore, a most dangerous task). There are fourteen girls from ten to sixteen years in the coke yard and six lads in the casting-house and refinery of from ten to fourteen years, some of whom get burned, but not too badly: there are a few girls at the mines, working below; they all work twelve hours a day and the furnaces and refineries work all night."

The Birth of a Novel

It was a new experience for Alexander Cordell to have another writer work closely with him on a project and I was delighted to help in any way I could to provide him with background research and suggestions for possible locations and historic incidents that might be included in his story. As a result we had telephone conversations several times a week and the following extracts from our correspondence will help to show how the book gradually took shape.

> 11th September 1985
> Castletown
> Isle of Man

Thanks for your letter of the 7th Sept.. I am glad to hear that you got back safely - I'm not surprised that you had a bumpy flight; the wind was very bad about the time you went off.

I've tried to phone you to congratulate you on the reviews you sent me; they are amazingly good and you could not have had a better initial reception of CORDELL COUNTRY. Donnie and I are delighted for you.

Your idea of preceding RAPE OF THE FAIR COUNTRY is one I have never considered; the idea is excellent, and appealing - very important!

Jethro, for me is the least attractive character; he was always a second best to Iestyn in my heart and third best to Hywel - who is the tops. Jethro is out - I've had enough of him, but Hywel? Yes I like that idea.

Congratulations again on your industry and creativeness. You deserve every success that the book will bring you - including posterity.

> * * * * * * *

> 7th September 1985
> Llanfoist
> Abergavenny

Dear Alex,

I am writing to send you some thoughts on the proposed new book which may be helpful to you.

Dating the life of Hywel Mortymer and his family

Iestyn would have been born in 1820, for in 1826 he is six years old. Hywel is 39 in 1826 so he was born in 1787 and would thus have been

20 years old in 1807. Morfydd is 16 in 1826 so she was born in 1810 when Hywel was 23.

Hywel Mortimer's father could have a farming background in the Lampeter/Llandovery area.

Location Ideas

You could somehow bring in the Gold Mines at Dolaucothi, near Pumsaint and then move the story south to the new industries of the Welsh Valleys. Hywel would have to end up in Blaenafon, but I think that it would be good to also bring Tredegar and Beaufort into the story. It is relevant that Crawshay Bailey took over the ironworks at Beaufort and one needs to bring in a link here to explain why in *Rape of the Fair Country*, Hywel is on Bailey's books.

Historic Events

(1) The termination of the Napoleonic Wars in 1815 resulted in the cease of a demand for arms. This caused widespread depression in the iron industry and the ironmasters, in 1816, decided to reduce wages in order to undercut their rivals in the Midlands. As a result riots broke out.The strikes and marches that took place then were a prelude to the Chartists uprising in South Wales.

(2) In 1816 there was rioting in Tredegar and soldiers were drafted there. They were billeted in the newly built workhouse. Night attacks were being made on various properties belonging to the Tredegar Ironworks Company and attempts made to wreck the Sirhowy tramroad. Guards were posted everywhere, but still the attacks continued.

(3) When the proprietors of Tredegar Ironworks gave notice to their workmen that a reduction in wages was to take place the men became angry and desperate. A large crowd of them proceeded to Merthyr to learn of the feelings of the men there. The Dowlais Ironmaster heard of their approach. Special Constables were sworn in and armed with pikes. They were positioned in a pass adjoining the works, near the dwelling of Ironmaster Guest.

(4) The Tredegar men seized the pikes from the special constables and broke them into pieces and the constables fled. The rioters proceeded to the works and shut down the furnaces. They then went on to other works in Merthyr.

(5) They then returned to Tredegar and Sirhowy and by this time their numbers had increased to several thousand. Crossing the hill to Beaufort, they found that the workers there were happy with their

employers, even though the wages were low. They then marched on to the works of Messrs Harford in Ebbw Vale. The blast furnace was stopped and more men joined them but no violence took place.

(6) From there, they proceeded to Blaenafon Ironworks. Thomas Hill reasoned with them and offered temporary relief. The men were starving and asked for food. He supplied them with beer but surprisingly they refused to drink it, preferring to remain sober. They remained at the works all night, stopping the blast furnaces. Next day they proceeded to the Llanelly Furnace in the Clydach Gorge and acted in the same manner. (It would be good for Clydach Gorge to be brought into the tale for the Ironworks there is now being excavated. I will take you there when you next come to Abergavenny).

(7) The men then marched over the mountains towards coal mines in the neighbourhood of Crumlin, Newbridge and Abercarn to learn of the workers' feelings in those places. Their numbers increased from 10 to 20,000, but as night came on they separated.

(8) The military were brought to Newport - then on to Merthyr in wagons - but no violence was offered from either side. The cavalry were sent from Cardiff but re-called. Some troops were sent to Pontypool and then on to Blaenafon. A troop of cavalry was even sent from Swansea.

(9) The eventual result of these events was that the ironmasters backed down and withdrew their notices of reduction in wages and the men returned to work.

(10) Another factor is the lack of food at this time. There was virtually a famine for the wheatcrop had been a failure and barley was so limited that the workers were prepared to work merely for food. Richard Fothergill (part owner of Tredegar and Sirhowy companies) bought all the barley he could and distributed it among his workers' families. He even set up a soup kitchen in his own house and supervised it himself!

The story needs to go right up to the birth of Iestyn and fit neatly into the beginning of *Rape of the Fair Country*. I feel sure that your readers would really appreciate such a link between the two books and the saga of the Mortymers would be considerably strengthened by this approach.

* * * * * * *

Thank you for your long and informative letter and your suggestions about the new book. We are leaving here on the 24th and will be in Abergavenny for the night of 26th September and again for three nights (28th-30th Sept). When we meet I'd like to talk in greater detail about the theme of the new book and its locale.

I agree with you that the book should begin in the Llandovery gold mines and then move to ironmaking in Gwent. The thing I have in mind is a virtual repeat of the RAPE theme and again with a family background. The 'togetherness' of the Victorian family seems to hit people in the heart.

But frankly at the moment I'm not very happy about continuing with the iron era: it has been my habit to take the trades one by one, as you know, and I've done iron pretty successfully. If Hywel could be employed on an off-shoot trade, in that area - say as a bailiff to Dan-y-Parc, for instance - or even a local blacksmith and perhaps working with mules and horses. (I knew a man who could whisper into the ear of a horse with astonishing effect). From there he could be pitchforked by calamity into iron, but I wish there was another completely different trade in that era, but short of an inn landlord I'm at sea on this. I know I'm wandering here, but this is the sort of letter it should be. In the end I think I'm going to be confined to an iron repeat, otherwise all our dreams are shot in the ankles. The timing is right as you have shown ably.

I'd like us to go to Tredegar and Beaufort while I am over and so immerse ourselves in evocation that wraiths appear; it can happen. The gold part is easy; it could be so enriched by the magic wand of the Romans that it could be highly informative as well as enjoyable. The industrial part is more difficult since I have done it so successfully before, and anything I do will tend to repeat even agriculture I have covered in HOSTS OF REBECCA.

But if it is going to be iron, then I am obliged to you for your intense research into the new areas; there is nothing in your thesis with which I quarrel; all is grist to this particular mill, and you have provided two distinct and interesting locales.

In RAPE, Hywel is a demi-god, and this aspect has to be preserved. This is best done by sympathy, and his exploitation in childhood and his noble sacrifices for his brood of followers must emphasise this. The reader who has read RAPE, and most will have done, will accept almost anything in his name, for his name is already magnetised. Then suddenly, through some tragic and terrible happening, they are all gone, and he is alone, without love or commitment.

Blaenafon could be an epic - a sort of Inn of the Seventh Happiness, the way beset with vagabonds and thieves. Inns where ghosts walk, sleeping with cattle, stealing food but no begging.

Perhaps in one extreme, the elder girl finds money ... only we know that she has sold herself at an inn. Remember SONG OF THE EARTH? That happening then, made an American publisher cry, believe it or not. Hywel knows, but holds and consoles her, and neither let on; they just watch the other children eat.

I continue to ramble on, and I am most grateful for all your help.

It was at this point that I wrote to Alex suggesting that Hywel Mortymer could be given noble ancestry.

Could not the Mortymers claim descent from the Mortimer family who married into the Owain Glyndwr family. Edmund Mortimer married Catrin, one of Glyndwr's daughters, after being captured at the Battle of Pilleth. He formed an alliance with Glyndwr and eventually died of starvation whilst defending Harlech Castle. The Mortimer ancestral home was at Wigmore Castle which was one of the most powerful fortresses in the Welsh Marches. It is of interest that Gwladys, the daughter of Llywelyn the Great also became the bride of a Mortimer. The noble Mortymers ruled the Marches of Wales for 400 years.

Two possibilities could be considered:-

(1) Hywel Mortymer could be descended from an illegitimate son of Sir Edmund Mortimer - perhaps from a possible relationship with a cousin, before his marriage to Catrin - the daughter of Owain Glyndwr.

(2) Alternatively the illegitimate child of Edmund Mortimer's nephew may have had a secret intrigue and the birth of that child was kept secret by the family of the young lady concerned.

Bear in mind that Sir Edmund Mortimer, when captured by Owain Glyndwr at the Battle of Pilleth, was persuaded to marry Owain's daughter Catrin, in return for his freedom. This ensured a pact between two great families. It is quite possible that Edmund Mortimer 'ditched' some noble young lady in order to marry Catrin. The female that he forsook may well have been pregnant with his child.

168

Alex replied:

25th September 1985
Isle of Man

Dear Chris,

Thanks for your letter and the 'lineage'. Your first and simplest idea is the best and it could work as follows:-

Edmund Mortimer married Glyndwr's daughter, true, but earlier had a liaison with a lady at his court; the son born to this girl was given the name Mortymer by Glyndwr, being 'on the wrong side of the blanket' and to hush the scandal. This child, a son, then married into full Welsh blood and the line became servants at court; slowly the 'royalty' died out and the Mortymers became peasantry with English-Welsh origins.

Do you think this works? You see I must keep it absolutely simple; nor must I labour the romantic thesis that Hywel is of noble blood, for it is going over the top.

5 November 1985
Isle of Man

I am developing through the tale a dark factor which eventually dominates the ending. You may recall that in *Rape of the Fair Country*, Jethro was splashed by iron and nearly killed; Edwina was murdered (her assailant never found) and that Hywel eventually met a violent death at the furnaces. Now, it could be that the Mortymers are under threat and by making the matter a vendetta I can obtain another dimension into the story.

The book opens with Hywel and his father travelling by coach when they are attacked; the driver and Hywel's father are killed and Hywel is left for dead. There is a storm raging and it will be an action opening. I shall have Hywel watching his father, half drunk and snoring in the coach, a man he hardly knows - grieving for his mother etc.

I think it would work. Do you? Perhaps I keep asking you because I've got internal doubts that it does?... !

I replied a few days later:

Dear Alex,

Many thanks for your letter and synopsis. I am reading it with great interest.

Regarding the Mortymer background as you outline - I see no problem with the idea - and it would not be possible for anyone to argue with it. Also I like the coach attack, for it provides a dramatic beginning to the novel and also provides a good way of disposing of Hywel's father.

A vendetta against the Mortymer family will work very well as a theme that could run through the book. Cast aside your doubts, for I am sure that you are on the right lines.

I would like to show you an excitong mountain road that runs from Tregaron to Abergwesyn, and is famous for a steep winding descent known as the 'Devil's Staircase' which could be an ideal location for your coach accident .

30th January 1986
Isle of Man

Dear Chris,

I suggest that we take two cars to the Cambrian Mountains on Sunday 23rd. We'll go to Brecon where Donnie will drop off and spend the day with Meg, the lady you met before: you can park your car there and the three of us will then go off to the 'Devil's Staircase' etc. That evening Donnie and I will take Meg out for a meal as we always do and presumably you'll go back to Abergavenny.

Next day, the Monday, which you say you will have off work, I'd like to share your company on the more particular research at Sirhowy and Tredegar; for this reason, Donnie is again doing her own thing - visiting friends in Abergavenny. When you and I return there I'll pick Donnie up and you may like to come with us for an evening meal, perhaps at that Chinese restaurant.

I thought I'd lay out a programme early so we could make appropriate arrangements at our leisure. We should have time enough to cover the ground we have in mind.

12th February 1986
Isle of Man

Dear Chris,

Thanks for your letter. I'm glad that the timings suit you, and I hope we can have a good day out there; novel journeyings can denegrate into travelogues if one isn't careful, so I want the trip brief in terms of time, but rich enough in terms of drama to hold itself up and perhaps lay the childhood characteristics of the early people. More and more I see this, as I laze with it, as a triumph of love over adversity; to conceive five hundred feet down in a three foot muddy level is one thing; for that love to shine like a diamond, and to bring forth a child with nobody to comfort you but your lover could be magnificent.

You can't talk to everyone like this, of course, and there, perchance could be the weakness of it all. Mao used to say that he heard the groan of every woman in labour, but I doubt if he did; he was usually too busy catching fleas in the waistband of his trousers. In the end I suppose it is we, not the politicians or the general public who suffer.

I would like you to do the talk in Blaenafon for me because somehow I have got to fit in a trip to Gibraltar and, possibly if Donnie and I are both still fit - to Hong Kong with Yang and Jenny later in the year, which, counting it all, means an awful lot of travelling for two old pensioners. I believe that your contribution is so total that nobody can add to it.

Got to go. All the best. Will be in touch with anything outstanding.

Alex in due course arrived in Abergavenny and early on Saturday morning we drove up to Abergwesyn, where we first located the *Old Grouse Inn* (now a private house), which he wanted to bring into his story. We then drove up the mountain road towards Tregaron for Alex to experience the dramatic scenery and the steep ascent known as the Devil's Staircase. It was his first visit to this area and he was very impressed and excited by everything he saw.

He particularly wanted to identify a suitable spot on this narrow mountain road where the coach could be attacked and pushed down into a ravine. This incident in the novel reads as follows:

"Now the coach skidded precariously on the flooded road and the two horses beat their hooves in a quieter, rhythmic pattern: rubbing at the misted window, I stared out over the dull forbidding country fifty feet below; one false hoof could send us somersaulting down into the flooded river."

171

The *Old Grouse Inn* at Abergwesyn is now a private house

The mountain road from Abergwesyn to Tregaron

The coach comes to a halt at a road block where three men are waiting and they tip the vehicle over the edge of the road. It tumbles down a steep bank to land on the edge of the river far below.

> "I saw below me the foaming Cledan River in full spate twenty feet down: flying hooves I saw, and a single spinning wheel, and felt my father's arms go about me as a lantern flared and we dropped into space.
>
> Now, locked in his embrace, I somersaulted in a mad world of scarlet and gold; into a topsy-turvy crescendo of thumps and smashes and pain: in a jack-in-the-box coffin we struck impeding rocks in our downward plunge, upright one second, upside down the next, but my father, not I, was taking the impact of the collisions. And then, in one last explosion of pain and light, the coach crashed into the mud of the river bank: glass tinkled, I remember, as I drifted into silence."

His father is killed, but Hywel manages to escape from the wreckage and he *"climbed from crag to crag and reached the berm of the Llandovery road; to sink sobbing, at the foot of the gibbet that bore the white mare's skull."*

With the *"sun rising over the mountains,"* Hywel makes his way to Pumsaint and the old *Cothi Inn*. But his enemies are on his trail and in order to hide from them he takes a job hauling trams in the old gold mines at Pumsaint.

The *Dolaucothi Inn*

Alex had not seen the gold mines before and we spent an hour or so wandering around the site and looking into some of the long abandoned levels. It was some years later that the site was opened to the public and guided tours introduced.

The village of Pumsaint is named after 'five saints'. There is a tradition that they were quintuplets born to Cynyr Forfdrwch ap Gwran ap Cunedda and their names were Gwyn, Gwynno, Gwynoro, Ceitho and Cynfelyn. There is a legend that these five brothers came under the power of an enchanter who hid them in a cave where they fell asleep. They will awaken and return to this world when a pious Bishop rules the diocese.

Near the Roman Gold Mines is a strange stone in which the saints are alleged to have left their footprints. It is a square upright stone about 3 feet high with

The Five Saints Stone

hollows in its four faces. It has in reality been hollowed out by hand held stone hammers crushing the ore, and it may be said that it serves as a memorial to gold diggers through the ages, pre-Roman, Roman, Norman and others.

> *"Now the village of Pumsaint gets its name from a famous Standing Stone that commemorates the resting place of the five saints - Gwyn, Gwyno, Gwynore, Celnin and Ceitho - who once journeyed here: indeed, one can see on the stone the ground hollows of their shoulders. Later the Romans tunnelled the place for gold, constructing adits that burrowed into the hills, using Celtic labour working under the lash. On and off this prospecting had continued down the centuries."*

Traces of a Roman fort and civil settlement have been revealed by excavations at Pumsaint. The reason for their presence here was of course the gold mines at nearby Dolaucothi. This is the only known Roman gold mine in Britain and the second largest in the Roman Empire. It is a unique site. There is evidence that the mines were worked before the Romans arrived and they certainly lost no time in taking over these mines for exploitation began just five years after their conquest of Wales in 75AD.

It is the only place in this country where the Romans are definitely known to have mined gold and one of the main reasons why the armies of the Roman Emperors were so keen to subjugate Wales in the years after their arrival in Britain in AD43, was the desire of the Roman government to increase its supply of this precious metal. The other Roman gold mines in Europe were in Spain and in the Roman province of Dacia (modern Romania).

The tradition that the Romans established a fort on the site of the present day village of Pumsaint was proved by excavations in the early 1970s, on the site of the car park of the Dolaucothi Arms Hotel. The fort provided protection and a base for the skilled engineers involved in directing the mining operations. It remained in use until about AD140, when it was demolished and abandoned

The gold mined here was probably exported to the imperial mint at Lyons in France or perhaps Rome. As this was one of the most important mines in Roman Britain it is not surprising that it was guarded by a fort. Various Roman gold ornaments have been found near the mines, including a solid gold chain. Plenty of Roman coins have also been discovered including a large hoard of coins.

Gold bearing pyrites wasextracted by means of open cast workings and underground galleries reaching a depth of 130 feet. The galleries were drained by a timber water wheel and a fragment of it can be seen in the National Museum at Cardiff. Large quantities of water used to treat the ore were brought to the site by three aqueducts cut into the hillside. Remains of aqueducts and reservoirs can still be seen. One of the aqueducts is stone-lined and seven miles in length.

In 1762 three thousand Roman medals were discovered here. Other items which can be seen in the British Museum, include a golden necklace, rings, and other jewellry of fine workmanship.

The mines were worked again in the 19th century and also during the 1930's. In 1941, the 2,577 acre Dolaucothi Estate, consisting of farmland and woodland, was given to the National Trust by Mr H.T.C. Lloyd Johnes as a memorial to his family who had owned it since the time of Henry VIII.

The Dolaucothi Goldmines are situated off the A482 Llanwrda to Lampeter road, within the 120 hectare Dolaucothi Estate. The site is now a National Trust visitor centre with underground tours available, led by experienced guides, who at all stages, explain the geological and historical background to the mines.

Dolaucothi is the only known Roman gold mine in the UK, and the only chance to see the lost gold mining heritage of Wales

Visitors panning for gold

"Ragged men, women and children were labouring in the red light, shovelling up the broken ore the miners were digging out of the adits, and spreading it for crushing under the hammers: then the milled stone was sprayed with water to catch the specks of gold and channel it down to the trappers: isolated groups of little children, the end of the night shift, were on their knees over puddling holes, wearily jigging reed baskets into pools of Cothi water."

"The trams did not run on wheels on a line, but on skids; bumping and carving a groove in the mud which greased their path.... the foal worked low, with a chain between his legs; the half-marrows pushed behind, their bare feet splayed to the rock crops; head bent, one arm hanging to the ground for purchase. No identifiable words accompanied the haul, only sighs and grunts and groans: gasping in the dust-laden air as they went, one tram after another; the draught donkeys called humans who had been hauling in this adit since the start of civilization.

But these were slaves to a modern purpose; the economic boom that plundered their strength for the profits of present day Romans; a new, baser breed of old speculators who hung their bullion on the backs of the younger generation; and who, had the law allowed them, would have had them under the whip."

Cordell only has Hywel working in the gold mines for a very brief time for he is discovered by his enemies and takes flight to follow the road to Llandovery. Whilst there, he goes to the church to visit the grave of his mother which bears the following inscription:

> *Lady Jane Mortymer (née Mortimer)*
> *Born August 13th 1760, died June 1st 1798*
> *Beloved wife of Hywel Iestyn Mortymer of Tregaron House daughter of Lord and Lady Mortimer of Llandovery*

St Dingad's Church, Llandovery

Hywel then walks to Trecastle where he joins up with Bimbo, a young lad who is heading for Blaenafon in the hope of finding employment in iron and coal. They travel on via Talybont and Trefil, where:

"... the great stone quarries that sent their limestone to the furnaces of the Top Towns , ... where iron was moulded into shape - Sirhowy and Tredegar, Merthyr Tydfil and Beaufort, Ebbw Vale and Nantyglo. From our high vantage on the edge of this lunar country we could see long lines of horses and carts coming and going along the Rassau stone-road that soon would become a tram road.

Pack mules and horses, each loaded with three-hundredweight panniers - the rough pig iron straight from the Sirhowy furnaces - were trudging, linked by a tethering rope, in long lines of misery to forging mills of works like that at Glangrwyney; there to join the canal and tram-road for shipment to the ports of the world."

Walking on they reach the area between Brynmawr and Blaenafon, *"a place of stunted trees and scraggy bushes bent into crippledom by the winds of the Coity mountain; itself a coal hill honeycombed by generations of miners and delvers since the start of Time."*

"Never will I forget the sight as we neared Blaenafon, the colours of the lonely bloomeries shooting their rockets to the stars."

"... music was coming from the Whistle Inn where off shift workers thronged; a man was singing a plaintive song in Welsh, his voice bass and pure on the wind: the pace of industry quickened as we neared the Brynmawr Corner and turned down North Street into Blaenafon. And such was the flashing and baying of furnace glare that I thought it was the end of the earth."

"The Drum and Monkey pub sign was creaking in the wind, and beyond this anxious-looking women with babies in shawls were looking at the food in the Company Shop window, which was filled with sausages and pies. Maimed beggars with skeletal children in their laps were squatting on the road opposite Staffordshire Row, this being built, we were told, for incoming Midland specialists who knew the colour of the flame; ostlers and farriers were to live here, too..."

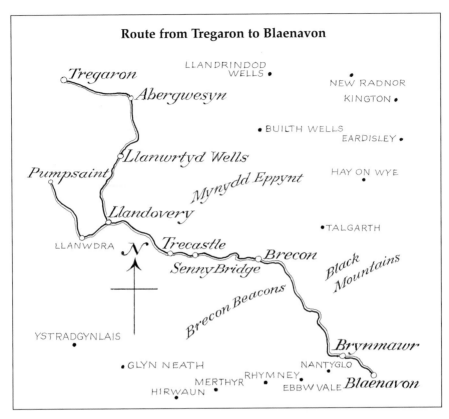

Route from Tregaron to Blaenavon

Tregaron

LLANDRINDOD WELLS •

Abergwesyn

NEW RADNOR

KINGTON •

• BUILTH WELLS

EARDISLEY •

Llanwrtyd Wells

Pumpsaint

Mynydd Eppynt

HAY ON WYE
•

Llandovery

• TALGARTH

LLANWDRA

Trecastle

Brecon

SennyBridge

Black Mountains

Brecon Beacons

YSTRADGYNLAIS
•

Brynmawr

• GLYN NEATH

NANTYGLO

RHYMNEY

MERTHYR •

• EBBW VALE

Blaenavon

HIRWAUN •

"Now we were in Fforest Fach, south of Senny and to the east of Crai, and that night we stripped off and bathed in the old Senni and the stars were as big as lanterns, the moon a fractured opal in the big black sky.

Later, near dawn, south of Brecon in the foothills of the Allt Ddu, we rested again because I had blisters, and the trees above us were a black tracery of branches against a sky of fleece, with Orion beaming searchlights and Sirius making her archeries of red and gold."

"Now, a day later, miles further east and free of the pursuing Mortimers, we found the land bathed in a magical brightness as we washed away the dust and dirt beneath drooping willow trees: the lake called Tal-y-Bont, iron flat to a sheeny loveliness, sparkled silvedr in the hot June day: wading deeper through the shallows, I dived, seeing a new world of wavering fauna and flowers, and rose into sunlight, spraying water."

"Two days later, coming over the top of a moonscape land called Trefil, it was like walking on the roof of the world."

181

Dear Chris,

I am grateful for the map you sent me, and in time, for what I am doing - the boys have just arrived at Garndyrus and met Selwyn ap Pringle, the miser of the Royal Oak! He has a daughter called Poll Plenty...It is now flying ahead, with joy.

I'd be obliged for a ' later' map, but have learned a lot from the one you enclosed. I am going to start Hywel working in a drift mine at Pwll-du, towing trams. I will send you some sample extracts shortly.

"Welcome to the Royal Oak, lads - Selwyn ap Pringle at your service," and he spat at our feet, "Is it ale and women you're after?"
"It is not, it's work," said I.

"Cross the road, go round the Tumble, ask for Mr Effyn Tasker - he's the overman round the Pwll-du drifts - and say Selwyn sent you."

"On all fours I rode the towing chain, bracing my toes on the stone sleepers for a purchase, and Bendy, his body as rigid as a bar, pushed behind."

"Some of the children never saw daylight, but worked underground, ate underground and slept in conditions where no decent master would have kept pigs.

They were run over by trams in darkness where they fell asleep at the brattice doors; crushed by runaway journeys, trapped in foul air pockets (we didn't know it was gas in those days). They were thrashed for eating in employer's time or dozing on the job."

Drammer Girls are employed for the filling and drawing of the drams (trams), of coal or iron-stone; it requires great strength. One 13 year old girl stated, "The work is very hard, the mine is wet where we work, and the workings are only 30 to 33 inches high." Her 11 year old sister said, "When we draw the drams, which contain 4 to 5 hundredweight of coal from the coal face to the main road, I make 48 to 50 journeys."

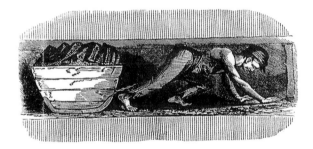

"I've been working down here three months dragging carts loaded with coal from the coal face to the main road underground; there are no wheels to the cart. It is not so well to drag them as the cart sometimes is dragged on to us, and we get crushed often. I have often hurt my hands and fingers and had to stay home."

Ben Thomas
aged 8

"The Marquis of Abergavenny, whose seat was at Neville Hall, converted to his possession 12,000 acres under the Enclosure Act. Evicting tenant farmers, he leased this land to Messrs Hopkins, Hill and Pratt, speculators who sunk £40,000 into its potential, realizing it was a source of ironstone, timber for charcoal, coal and limestone - the ingredients in great demand for war.

So Pwll-du sprang up, and was peopled by immigrant Irish, English, and evicted Welsh farmers and labourers, and this gave the village a soul.

Upper Row, a terrace of fourteen cottages, was built, followed by Lower Row, one of twenty-eight cottages: two public houses followed - the Lamb and the Prince of Wales, later becoming the Company Shop. St Catherine's Church came next, then a little chapel called Horeb, and the community thrived. Drifts and levels were sunk and the coal was good. And while Mr Effyn Tasker bossed the output here, it was in the chapel that Tomos Traherne held court."

Upper Row and the Lamb Inn Pwll-du - drawing by Michael Blackmore

184

"Women took their place with men in 1800; later they were banned from underground by Parliamentary Acts which most employers ignored; it was the same with the employment of children in the mines. Nobody, not even the children, knew their ages in many cases, since there was no official registration of birth; a girl of five could say she was ten if her parents needed the money. The employers took advantage of this; two children aged ten could do the work of a man and take home a quarter of his money."

"In all the Top Towns of Wales, from the Crawshays of Cyfartha to the Reverend Monkhouse of Sirhowy, were small armies of children; even animals took preference to the battalions of urchin young who, driven by hunger, besieged the iron towns: here they were cornered, given a shilling for the bait tin, and taken on in droves."

"Mines, iron compounds, drifts and levels opened and engulfed them in a score of trades, from rag-cleaners to mule-skinners, ore-scrabblers to tub-trammers: and the normal shift was twelve hours, at a ha'penny an hour. Some of these children never saw daylight, but worked underground, ate underground and slept in conditions where no decent master would have kept his pigs."

"We are working at the Forges labouring about the place, cleaning, sweeping, wheeling iron and other work. We work under the Company from six to six, but we are allowed meal times and sometimes go home for dinner. We get 5s per week; we do not work at night - none of the girls do - but some of the pilers work at night. There are about 30 girls big and little about the Forges; we are about the youngest. There are not more than a dozen under 13 years old. We work very hard, but do not work in hot places. The work agrees with our health very well. We sometimes lose days, but not often from sickness. We have not been in day school, but sometimes go to Sunday School."

Mary Jones aged 13
and Elizabeth Hall aged 14

This drawing by William Byrne, based on a sketch by Sir Richard Colt Hoare (1799), shows a covered bridge supported by ten arches, which have been converted into workers' dwellings

Hywel is now living under one of the bricked up arches of an old viaduct, built to carry a railroad leading into a mine.

> *"And since workers' housing was in short supply with the rush of incoming immigrants, Mr Hopkins bricked up the bridge arches and turned them into homes: secure against all weather: whole families were raised in this accommodation: folks like Mrs Ten Beynon's Irish mother, who raised fifteen children. In Number One Bridge Arches, which was ruled by Ma Corrigan, lived some of the labouring children, including me, the eldest."*

The more important workers were housed in specially built cottages:

> *"Staffordshire Row for the Midland iron specialists and Shepherd's Square for the puddlers and refiners, were completed that year."*

> *"... Stack Square, warmer than most, being near the furnaces, had underground tunnels dug for cottage heating, and they were the cosiest rooms in town - the furnace gases, hot from the engine blast, first circulated in the tunnels before going up the stack."*

Stack Square adjoins Blaenafon Ironworks

"Number One Stack Square... was the official company office. Here were weighbridge clerks in shiny suits, red noses and starched collars: shillings jingled in the hands of the lofty paymaster; an enormous safe in a corner had KEEP OUT written on the door.

Here were produced the tally-cards and receipts; how much coal, iron and limestone poured into the furnaces since a week last Monday. Here, too was fiddled the prices in the Company Shops in Stack Square, up at Pwll-du and behind the Drum and Monkey."

"Stack Square was communally heated. The engineers knew what they were about in our time. By positioning the main smoke chimney within three sides of a square and building the workers' cottages around it, there wasn't a room in those cottages unheated, except in strike time."

The Clydach Gorge

Dear Chris,

I've just tried to phone you, but you were not in, so I'm getting this down on paper, because I will be out myself tomorrow.

I am now needing more information on Clydach. Can you give your thoughts to possible locations to bring in when you can? Otherwise, proceeding well and now on Chapter twenty. It has really taken off, yet for me lacks that close harmonic 'intimacy' of telling which RAPE possesses, despite all my efforts to manufacture it. Can't really think why, except that it isn't so clever to swim the Channel again when once you've successfully been in the public eye, but the child labour aspect is terrifying.

I expect you are out lecturing somewhere. Too tired to write anymore. Hope all is well with you.

4th August 1986
Isle of Man

Dear Chris,

Thanks, for the Clydach Notes, which are most valuable, and they came in time, for I'd just turned away from the Black Death in Sirhowy and headed for Clydach; a rather beautiful if earthy love scene occurs (and for the first time, a consummation) in the gorge. And Shadrach and Mesdach (with their embalmed grandpa Abednigo in a chair upstairs) have arrived in the Prince of Wales (Clydach) from the old Cothi Inn just in time.

Bendi has died. The first hunger march of 1801 is over, Sam Hill and Aaron Williams hanged at Cardiff; six others with them, forty to transportation, others sent to the Usk Correction. And Hywel's love for Rhian is flowering into perfection.

The vendetta is on: Tom Mortymer is seen in a Yeomanry charge at Nantyglo...Sometimes I nearly weep that it is so dead; other times I nearly weep because it is so alive. The author is always like a betrayed lover, the last to know! Thank you for your help and good luck for your new book.

Lower part of the Clydach Gorge, with Sugar Loaf in background

One morning, in early September I picked Alex up at his hotel in Abergavenny and we drove to the Clydach Gorge. Turning off the A465 we followed the road leading to Clydach village. "I know nothing about this valley, it is all new to me." said Alex.

I drove into the picnic site car park, and said, "First of all I want to show you the excavation work that has recently been carried out on the site of the Clydach Ironworks, which could certainly be brought into the story."

We walked a short way up the road, crossed a little stone bridge and followed a track to the left beside the fast flowing river Clydach. Shortly we reached a cast iron bridge spanning the river.

Alex was immediately impressed, and asked when it was constructed. I then pointed out the date 1824 which can be seen on one of the iron girders and said, "It is called Smart's Bridge - just who Smart was I have no idea, but this early cast iron bridge was built to link the Clydach Ironworks with the Company offices which stood on this side of the river. They were demolished when the Heads of the Valleys Road was built.

We crossed the bridge and reached the site of the old ironworks where some men were working on the excavation which was being undertaken on behalf of Blaenau Gwent Borough Council.

Smart's Bridge was built in 1824

I introduced Alex to their supervisor Anne Wilson a young recently qualified archaeologist. She told us that they had begun the excavation a few months previously and that she was finding it a very exciting project. She was looking forward to revealing as much as possible of the works which was first established in about 1795.

The Clydach Ironworks was excavated by a Job Creation team in 1986

This works was originally operated by the Hanbury family of Pontypool until 1797, when the widow of John Hanbury leased the concern to Edward Frere and Thomas Cooke, who also leased adjoining land from the Duke of Beaufort. Three years later they formed a partnership with Edward and John Kendall of the Beaufort Ironworks and this resulted in the Clydach Ironworks Company being formed.

Edward Frere sank thousands of pounds into the development of the works but further finance for the undertaking was always lacking. In 1803 Walter and John Powell joined the Company and introduced more capital. The partnership then went under the name of Frere, Cooke and Powell.

By 1809 Thomas Cooke had retired and John Powell had passed away leaving George Frere and a new partner John Jones in control of the works. George Frere was a hard worker who had a high regard for his employees and generally treated them well.

Reconstruction of Clydach Ironworks by Michael Blackmore

From the ironworks, we walked up a short incline to reach Clydach village where several terraced cottages once housed ironworkers and quarrymen employed by the Clydach Ironworks Company. Alex suggested that we should try and have a conversation with the oldest resident that we could find. After knocking on a door we were directed to the home of a spritely 90 year old lady who welcomed us into her kitchen.

She was delighted to meet Alexander Cordell, having read *Rape of the Fair Country* several times and the kettle was soon boiling for cups of tea. Alex asked her to tell him about her earliest memories of living in Clydach and she told us with obvious pride of her long life there and how the stone quarry had been the main source of employment for the men of the village.

For me it was fascinating to see how Alex went about his research, by chatting to elderly folk to obtain little anecdotes, both sad and humourous that he could possibly stitch into his novels.

The ironworks had closed long before this lady was born but tales of men working there had been handed down through the generations and we were able to gain a picture of life in this little village as it would have been in the early years of the twentieth century.

Stone cottages in Clydach, once occupied by quarrymen and ironworkers

We then left Clydach and drove up to the *Drum and Monkey Inn* which is higher up the gorge on the old road to Brynmawr. As we walked past the pub I commented to Alex, "This pub used to be called the *Prince of Wales* and when the name was changed to *Drum and Monkey* a few years after *Rape of the Fair Country* was published, it caused much confusion. People who had read the novel, but were not familiar with the area believed that this was the pub mentioned in the book and not the one of the same name that used to be in North Street Blaenafon."

Alex laughed and replied," Yes, I didn't know whether to be amused or annoyed, but really I saw it as a compliment, for it was an indication to me that people were fascinated by everything to do with *Rape of the Fair Country*. It is a great shame of course that the Blaenafon *Drum and Monkey* pub in Blaenafon no longer exists."

The *Drum and Monkey Inn*, Clydach Gorge

Just past the pub, I led the way down to a subway which took us underneath the Heads of the Valleys road and we then descended some steps into the depths of the Clydach Gorge.

Alex then remarked, "This is all new to me and I am intrigued to know where you are taking me."

I then replied, "We are going down to the Devil's Bridge which is an exciting location that you might like to bring into your story. It has a very special atmosphere and there is even a long standing tradition that William Shakespeare once came here and found inspiration for his play "Midsummer Night's Dream."

194

The Devil's Bridge in the depths of the Clydach Gorge

Standing on the middle of the old stone bridge we looked down a tumbling waterfall into the bottom of the narrow gorge. I pointed out a rock on the left in which, with a bit of imagination, the Devil's face can be seen. Below the waterfall is a pool called Pwll y Pwcca which translates as Puck's Pool and further down is Shakespeare's Cave. The tradition that the Bard came here is certainly very strong.

The face of the Devil can be seen in a rock below the Devil's Bridge

We crossed the bridge and then walked up the river bank a short distance. I then pointed to a rock surrounded pool near the far side of the river. "There is a pool over there which is known as the 'Whirley Hole' and there is a local superstition that it is bottomless. In reality it is the resurgence of water flowing from the Llangattock caves and this has been proved by dye testing."

"There is even a dubious tale of a dog entering the caves at Llangattock and re-emerging here in the Clydach Gorge. I have also heard stories of people long ago committing suicide by drowning themselves in the pool. A tale is also told of a man who once came here to drown his unwanted dog. But the man slipped into the pool and drowned while the dog went home."

Alex then commented, "It really is a fascinating place and I may well find a use for it to provide a tragic end to one of my characters. I had no idea that the Clydach Gorge was so enchanting. It has been a marvellous experience just to come here."

Clydach Gorge in the vicinity of the Drum and Monkey Inn

"In the year that Rhia and I came, Clydach had already been vandalised by incoming industrialists who, discovering its mineral wealth, saw not beauty, but a source of profit.

They stripped the forests of trees to make charcoal for their furnaces; they felled the great pines to make coffins for their workers, who by drinking Clydach's now polluted water, died of typhoid, scarlet fever and cholera. While the Hanbury's initiated the Vale's violation, it was the Freres who tolled its death knell. Iron-making demands ironstone, fuel and limestone, and Clydach possessed these in plenty. To facilitate their removal, tram-roads began to criss-cross the fair land like bleeding veins, viaducts spanned the ravines, tunnels were bored into the hills, streams dammed and broken on the wheel."

"Taverns and alehouses sprang up - the Prince, an iniquitous inn on the Black Rock, the Forgehammer and the Navigation Inn on the new canal. Into these the workers crowded to escape in tipsy dreams the sweated labour and the stink of sulphur."

Forge Row is situated close to the river Clydach

Hywel is now employed as a top-filler for the furnaces at Clydach Ironworks, *"the most dangerous job in ironmaking."* His wife Rhia becomes *"a cinder girl, a guarantee to destroy the lungs."*

They settle into No 1 Forge Row, on the end of twenty terraced cottages, situated between the Clydach river and the road, near the new tinplate works and the furnace compound.

> *"In front of Forge Row was the Clydach River that turned the giant waterwheel for the Llanelly Mill, and tripped the drop-hammers. Just over the way were the stables, and the farriers kept us awake with their shoeing and hammering: a branch tram-road connected us with the Office. So, what with the roaring of the furnaces under blast, the hammering in the tin works, and the ringing of the anvils, trying to get to sleep was a major occupation."*

> *"Clydach Vale thrived sending its iron down the canal to Newport. With the third furnace now at work and the compound loaded with trammers, barrow-men, butties, puddlers and refiners, there was more commotion than at a Connemara pig-fight."*

Filling the furnaces was very dangerous work

"The Great Wheel, competing with Merthyr's wheel of later years, whirred above the pouring leat that spun it; then roared the work-out water down the Gorge to the foaming Cascader and the tripping bellows of the wooden launder. Some say they could hear it thundering down in Abergavenny."

"Twenty feet above the great compound the charging house was mobbed with filler-gangs; the barrow-handlers scampering like pygmies against the glow. We worked silently, leaving to the furnaces their bellowing as we stuffed their hot bellies with ore, lime and coal."

"... the furnace roared; I saw Guto's boots go up as he slipped under the load, and fell head first into the boiling iron. The molten bubbling sprayed up in white arms, as if to catch him. In a two-second fuzz he blazed, did Guto; the blaze shut off his shriek as the steam of him whisped past me. When I looked again the barrow was still there, precariously tipping..."

The *Rock and Fountain Inn*

Hywel loses his job and, desperate for somewhere to live, he and Rhia move into a little barn near the *Rock and Fountain Inn*. Hywel is penniless and with a pregnant wife he needs money desperately. One night, leaving Rhia asleep in the barn, he sets off to make a quick sovereign.

Climbing Gilwern Hill, he passes through Pwll-du in the dark and makes his way to a remote hollow known as the Punchbowl, on the north side of the Blorenge, where he knows that a prize fight would be taking place.

"Often, walking in the Usk Valley at dusk, I had seen a ring of lights burning on the slopes of the Punchbowl on the Blorenge Mountain; a prize-fight would be in progress, and this would herald the Special Constables and Militia from the Red Lion at Abergavenny, for prize fighting was illegal: it was up on the mountain that men like Big Rhys, Will Blaenafon and Dai Swipo earned good money."

A Moonlight Walk to The Punchbowl

Alex had just sent me the chapter in which he describes Hywel trying to win some money by participating in a prize fight at the Punchbowl and one dark evening I decided to walk to that location from my home in Llanfoist.

Below Llanfoist Wharf I entered the gloomy tunnel which burrows beneath the Monmouthshire and Brecon canal and tramped on with the noise of my boots echoing off the stone walls, accompanied by the sound of the stream roaring beside me down the 'Devil's Gully'. When one walks through this tunnel there is always a tendency to duck your head, despite the fact that for anyone who is less than six feet in height there is plenty of clearance.

This tunnel passes under the Monmouthshire & Brecon Canal

Emerging from the tunnel beneath the end wall of the old Wharfemaster's cottage, I headed up to a stile and was soon ascending the incline which rises steeply through the trees. A stream trickled down on the left and rooks were calling from the treetops as the dusk was falling.

The double lines of stones that once held the iron plateways firmly in place are now well and truly scattered. A few are still in their original positions, but many have been pushed into the stream or to one side of the track. This bottom section of the incline used to be known as the 'Big Drop' and it is about 300 yards in length. The incline was constructed in three stages and between each section was a platform where a brake wheel was situated to control the descent of the trams.

The Blorenge Mountain overlooks the historic market town of Abergavenny

The Punchbowl is a beautiful location on the north-east side of the Blorenge

I crossed a stile and continued up through the trees and on emerging from the wood headed up towards a fence directly above, where I reached another stile. On the other side, I paused to catch my breath and looked back on the dimming outline of Sugar Loaf, the twinkling lights of Abergavenny and Skirrid Fawr sitting like a grey dog in the background.

From there, I followed the fence to the left and then made my way along more level ground towards a hollow on the side of the Blorenge. It is known as the Punchbowl and by a strange coincidence this is indeed a fitting name, for years ago it was used as sort of hillside amphitheatre where mountain fighters and their supporters met in secret for illegal bare-fisted contests. I immediately thought of Hywel Mortymer:

> *"It was a Saturday night. Leaving Rhia asleep in the Rock and Fountain barn, I turned out to make a quick sovereign. Up to my elbows in my trews and with my collar turned against the biting wind, I set out for the mountain. Climbing Gilwern Hill, I went through Pwll-du in the dark. I saw a galaxy of lights, then further on, a small square of flaming torches. Slipping, sliding down the mountain, I reached the prize ring."*

> *"Heads turned to a new party approaching - that of the Marquis of Abergavenny come up with his young bloods from the Nevill Hall ball. Led by the Marquis, they came on horseback; most already tipsy from drinking and revelry with their paramours.."*

> *"The bell tolled like a gong of doom; with my fists held high as Dai Bando had taught me, I went out to meet the White Celt. He was quick. I knew it from the first blow of the fight, a swinging right that grazed my chin, and I slipped on the damp grass and went headlong. Instantly he was on top of me, his elbow sinking into the pit of my stomach, but I threw him off and came upright. Ducking and weaving, he came storming in with hooks to have my head off."*

> *"The crowd was roaring. I heard Big Rhys's voice and Dai Swipo's throat-punch soprano ringing above the cheering of the dandies. Money was chinked as new bets were laid: the body of my opponent was shining with sweat and his expression changed from surprise to pain as I circled him, shooting straight lefts through his guard, snapping his head back."*

My thoughts were rudely interrupted by a sheep suddenly popping up in front of me to scamper down the track bleating as she raced along. Other ewes then cried out in unison and the strange silence was immediately broken.

Soon I reached a gate, beyond which the track crossed a field and ahead I could make out Coed y Prior Wood, below which twinkled the lights of Llanelen.

The discordant shrieks of owls greeted me as I arrived at the Punchbowl. Then silence returned and I stood beside the tranquil pool gazing towards the steep and wooded hillside. Wishing to maintain the atmosphere of silence, I resisted the temptation to shout, to test the echo, which can be quite remarkable in the right atmospheric conditions.

Beyond the end of the man-made dam which was constructed some years ago by a local landowner to make the pool for fishing purposes, I reached a lane ascending beside a stone wall. An owl hooted directly above me as I pondered how many feet through the passing centuries had tramped along this track.

Once through the trees, I ascended a sloping field and at the top I used my torch to find a way down a bank into a sunken lane. It led me down beneath low branches along a thick bed of leaves to reach a gate. I continued with my torch picking out occasional stones and fallen branches on the sunken track.

Across to my left I noticed lights in a cottage window and a dog barked when his sharp ears picked up the sound of my movements. The lane descended with twists and turns and in one place I walked ankle deep through a long stretch of leaves. On reaching a gate and a farm drive, I headed down the road and then turned right with my boots now crunching on gravel. Ignoring a lane to the right I carried on to reach a T-junction, where I turned left and then crossed a stile by a footpath sign.

The path now led me across Coed y Prior Common to a stile at the top of a forestry plantation. With the distinctive smell of pine in my nostrils I followed a track carpeted with pine needles and in due course emerged onto a lane near two cottages.

The lane tunnelled steeply down through the trees and my torch suddenly picked out the glint of a '5 ton restriction' sign and I knew that I had reached a stone bridge spanning the canal. Crossing a stone stile I joined the towpath and made my way back to Llanfoist Wharf.

>>>>>>>>>>>>>>>>>>>>>>>>>>>>>>>>>>>>>>>

When Hywel returned to the *Rock & Fountain* barn he found that Rhia had gone to the Devil's Bridge in the Clydach Gorge. Hywel went in pursuit of her and found himself drawn towards a deep pool which is known as the 'Whirley Hole' and reputed to be bottomless.

"It was raining again, pelting down through the canopy of trees; only shafts of moonlight guided me now, the undergrowth was thinner as I neared the pool. And I heard, long before I saw it, the water-spout of resurgent flood water that drained the distant Llangattock caves: these, the honeycombing tunnels and cathedrals of emptiness born when the world was ice."

"The whirlpool, regurgitating, rose to the rim in a threat to engulf me, then sank low into its pit of blackness. The siphoning shrieked; the gravitation gurgled - I stared at the throat of the gorge as it sank and sucked, to rise again into a bulging pool of silence.

And I saw, in that silence, something flashing a colour in the centre of the vortex. Higher, higher it rose; now circling out into the lazier swims of suction, before being snatched back and tossed, drowning into the gush. Now momentarily it appeared again, and I saw it clearly before it finally sank. It was Rhia's little pink hat. "

The Whirley Hole in the bed of the river Clydach

Some Years Later

The story moves on to 1810, and Hywel is now about 24 years of age. He is employed as a puddler at Blaenafon Ironworks and living in lodgings in Staffordshire Row, North Street. Much respected as a gentleman puddler, he is a snappy dresser who earns good money and even owns a pony and trap. He decides that it is time that he found a new wife.

15th August 1986
Isle of Man

Dear Chris,

Elianor has now come into the tale, and I have chosen Ynysgau Chapel, at the entrance to 'China' in Merthyr (Hywel met her at Cyfarthfa Horse Fair if you recall, so presumably her father, a pastor was in service there...)

It now goes apace, but I don't know how good it is, only how big. A lot will depend on the success of the recast-rewrite, but however good or bad it is, nobody will allow me the accolade of putting RAPE in the shade; the public disallows such things; they take a book to their hearts and it becomes a first love - best love. Anyway, thanks for your continued help on research.

Got to go. Hywel is about to attend Ynysgau Chapel in the hope of seeing Elianor again. What a life ! I will be in touch.

One Sunday, Hywel is in Merthyr, attending evening service in Ynysgau Methodist Chapel and he has his eye on Elianor Jones, the youngest daughter of the Reverend John Jones .

"Elianor Jones stared straight ahead... her eyes occasionally slanting across to me to see if I was still keen.

This is love-making done with the eyes; the flicking glance and casual air: a clever old business under the piercing stare of a sixteen-stone father up in the pulpit and his voice rang out across the crowded heads.

... His eyes fixed upon mine and drilled to the back of my head; fierce and sweating this one, like a bear with a collar on. He'd make a queer old father-in-law, I reflected."

Two months later Hywel marries Elianor Jones at Ynysgau Chapel and takes her back to Blaenafon where they settle into No 5 Stack Square.

"As a gentleman puddler in the money I spared nothing to do her proud. ... gentry furniture; a table, two chairs, pink curtains at the window facing the furnaces; a good strong ball-topped bed with a horsehair mattress, and a rug for getting out on to a well-scrubbed floor..."

"I stood for a while watching and listening to the noises of my town. What is there, I wonder, in the sagging bricks and mortar of a little town that clutches at the heart? Like the Waun Mary Gunter, the Hill Pits cottages near Garn-y-erw; Stable Row where the farriers and ostlers lived, Engine Row where lived the engineers, and lovely St Peter's, the first real school on the mountains.

Ty-Fry, the gamekeeper's cottage up on Keeper's; the Pwcas over on Milfraen Moor, Elgham Farm where the Little People lived. The Ironworks Company Shop beside the Drum and Monkey, where shawled women ate bread through the glass in strike time; Dr Steel's surgery where Blackie Garn, the sin-eater, had his leg off twice. Regal St Peter's Church, where my son was later married; he who was as yet a quickening in Eleanor's womb.

Aye, what is there in a town that enmeshes the soul?"

A view down North Street showing a large number of buildings demolished during a period of slum clearance in the 1970s

Dear Chris

I am now entering a historical period of seething discontent. Starvation followed the ending of the Napoleonic Wars; and the iron towns in the Welsh mountains were the first to suffer; the period coincided with the advent of the new Poor Law, and as fast as the Government built the new workhouses, places which condemned the old and lame to a life of degradation - dividing wife from husband in separate living accommodation - so the workers attacked and destroyed them.

Workers' leaders sprang up everywhere, and as their violence escalated so governmental reaction became more severe: local militia units were formed by the gentry and aristocracy for their own protection since many of these iron-making communities were mountainous and too isolated for protection by military units as far away as Brecon and Swansea, and proof of this was given in the Bread or Blood riots of Merthyr when worker insurgents actually took the town and defended it against the attacking Highland and Yeoman regiments for three days. Here a hundred were killed and scores more wounded, and the Red Flag was raised in Britain for the first time. Fearing a repeat of the French Revolution, suppression was usually swift and unjust, as witness the hanging of the innocent Dic Penderyn, whose innocence I proved by Home Office documentation in *The Fire People*.

I will make Hywel Mortymer a leader in the fight for better social conditions. As a gentleman puddler, his position is privileged and he will use it to the best possible advantage. By night he is a grain-raider, capturing it from food columns and hiding it in mountain caves for distribution to the hungry.

What I want to do is to build up Hywel's character and explain his later political attitude when Morfydd becomes rebellious: he has been through all this before, and, with his efforts defeated by established thinking, has long abandoned them.

Inspired with the success of the French Revolution... emissaries of the New Republic were ranging over Europe, and the unrest of Wales's new frontier towns was attracting organised revolt. The riots of ten years before were now being reborn in the failure of harvest after harvest. And, while the owners were basking in the rush for armaments, the price of wheat went up again. The hanging of Samuel Hill, Aaron Williams, and others who inspired the 1800 marching gangs, had temporarily halted the revolutionary fervour. But now even the King was worried: the government sent spies into Wales to track down the sources of this new anarchy.

October 6th 1986
Isle of Man

Dear Chris,

I have been seriously thinking about the plot for the new book; if a theme is needed - yes, well a theme is bound to be needed - but a strong one, I mean, what better than HYWEL's activities against the exploitation of the child labour from which he so sadly suffered. I've been on to National Library and I'm getting on loan the Blue Books; also just received child-labour terrors from an old Chepstow friend - covering Lancashire in the mid 1840's - terrifying stuff. Yet Hywel sent his own son (Iestyn) early to work against Morfydd's advice - even this would be a   logical action if something in his struggle against child victims utterly changed his outlook. At the moment I'm a bit shy of an incident for the ending. I need something really good to finish the book, or it could fall flat in the kitchen of the house in Shepherd's Square.

Hywel attends a secret meeting on the side of Coity Mountain - not to discuss social benefits, nor the cost of Tommy Shop groceries - but the condition of the workers' children. The leader who speaks eloquently to the gathering urges the men to take action to stop the exploitation of their children:

"You and I, my friends, contributed to another evil by tolerating it: do not we ourselves take babies down the pits because another head means another tram, for money to pay our debts? Do not we stand and watch our sons and daughters thrashed for falling asleep at the tunnel doors?"

A few weeks later, I took Alex to Nantyglo to see the work that was being carried out by Gwent County Council, through a Job Creation Scheme to preserve the Round Towers which were built by the Bailey brothers on their estate in about 1820.

Their fine mansion Ty Mawr (Great House) had been built on an elevated but sheltered site and was approached through an avenue of trees and surrounded by large gardens. The building had a rather grand colonnaded front supported by six iron pillars cast in the Nantyglo Ironworks, and inside was a magnificent marble staircase.

But the Baileys must have felt uneasy in their great mansion after the Merthyr uprising of 1813 and in order to protect themselves and their families from their own workers in times of trouble, they constructed two fortified towers. It has even been claimed that they linked Ty Mawr with one of the towers by constructing an underground passage, but this has yet to be discovered. The towers were kept stocked with food and ammunition in preparation for a possible siege.

I introduced Alex to Trevor Rowsen, who was well known for his research into Nantyglo's history and had special knowledge of the Round Tower complex in particular. The two men subsequently became good friends and Trevor was frequently consulted by Alex when he was doing research for subsequent novels.

We examined the original iron door which is still in place in the North Tower. It could be fastened by two massive bolts and there are two holes through which muskets could be poked and swivel plates that could be moved to cover the openings at other times.

Climbing the sturdy stone steps set into the inner wall we emerged onto the roof of the tower which is made of slotted iron segments, all fitting into a central disc. Trevor commented that, "Iron was probably used because it was readily available from the local ironworks."

A considerable amount of iron was used in the construction of the towers and during the First World War the upper tower was partly dismantled in order to obtain scrap iron. It was a storey higher than the other one and my research has revealed that at one time Crawshay Bailey's secretary, James Wells, resided on the top floor with his wife and two daughters."

We then walked across to the massive stable block where the Baileys once kept their horses and carriages. Trevor commented, "I have found references to the fact that Redcoats were billeted for two weeks above the main stable block in 1822, when they were called to subdue local riots which were started by a combination of Nantyglo workers led by a certain Josiah Evans."

Reconstruction of Ty Mawr by Michael Blackmore

Alexander Cordell talking to Project Officer, Paul Wellington
on top of the southern Round Tower in 1986

The northern Round Tower at Nantyglo

The three of us agreed that the site which is in private ownership would have great potential as a visitor centre for tourists, with a fascinating story to be told and that it was most important for these unique buildings to be preserved.

Before departing, we walked down to the site of Ty Mawr where Crawshay Bailey had lived until 1850, when he retired to Llanfoist House in the Usk Valley. All that can be seen now is an excavated area with the foundations and cellars of the building well defined.

The verandah base still exists, along with the plinth base of one of the iron columns, and several kerb stones to correct the route of carriages hitting the verandah. In the front areas of the house can be seen the box-like structures of the foundations, showing something of the original room layoutof the building.

Towards the rear of the house are situated three large cellars complete with access steps to the courtyard and the kitchen areas. The servants were housed in the nearby Trosnant House (demolished) and at the rear of Ty Mawr were a series of annex buildings which enclosed a small coach yard.

Trevor commented, "This house was a typical Georgian layout and in its day would have been a magnificent building. It contrasted greatly with the workers' houses which were quite appalling. If we look across the valley we can see the remains of what was Bayliss's Row. These houses were constructed without windows on this side so that the occupiers would not be able to gaze across at their master's mansion. The mansion itself was built on made-up ground and it provided the Baileys with a southerly view while being well sheltered from the sounds and smells of the Works."

Alex then asked, "When was Ty Mawr last lived in and when was it demolished?"

Trevor replied, "The house was last occupied after Crawshay Bailey by a series of works managers. The last person to live here was Samuel Lancaster of Blaina. When he died in 1855, his body was taken from the house and put on a train to be taken for burial at Highgate. Within a month there was a sale of furniture and effects from the house. In 1900 it was still a substantial building and there was a proposal for it to become a hospital. But a Dr Bevan, who lived at Ty Meddig on the other side of the valley opposed the idea, claiming that it was too near an open sewer. Eventually Ty Mawr was demolished during the Second World War."

The southern Round Tower was used as a home for James Wells who was private secretary to Joseph and Crawshay Bailey. According to the 1841 census returns he lived on the upper floor.

In due course Alex included a brief mention of the Round Towers in the novel:

> *"I tethered the pony in the shadows: seeing in a sudden glow of molten iron, the Bailey's Round Towers; two great battlements they were building to protect them from their workers.*
>
> *These fortifications, like Fothergill's Folly in Sirhowy or Cyfartha Castle (soon to be erected in Merthyr), were the masters' replies to local hatred. The riots of 1800, 1816 and last year threatened not only their profits at a time of their workers' distress, but also their lives. The Roundhouses here, for instance, were to be stocked with arms and provisions to resist siege until military protection arrived from Brecon Barracks."*

Pointing across the valley Trevor said, "Over there you can see the first ironworks school built in 1828 by the Baileys. An inspector named Jeremiah Symonds called at the school in 1841. He recorded that there were 214 pupils on the books, but only 11 were in school that day. Out of the eleven, two of the children had limbs missing. But the headmaster assured the inspector that this was no problem for Crawshay Bailey had promised them employment at his works."

Leaving Nantyglo, we then drove back towards Blaenafon and decided to stop for lunch at the *Whistle Inn* near Garn-yr-erw. Alex had a special regard for this old pub and it features in *Rape of the Fair Country* when Iestyn Mortimer stopped there for a quick pint on the way to his wedding at St Peter's Church, Blaenafon.

While we were eating our meal, Alex asked me what I knew about the large area of bog called Waun Afon which lies just north west of the *Whistle Inn*.

I replied, "Well I certainly wouldn't want to try walking across it and I do happen to know that during the Second World War a Halifax bomber crashed into it and sank out of sight. It had been on a routine training flight and developed a problem. The pilot managed to manoeuvre it away from Blaenafon town and steer it towards this area of open country. The crew of seven all baled out and fortunately no one was killed." Alex nodded, "Yes, I have heard that story as well and I intend to bring the bog into my story for it is a good place for one of Hywel's enemies to come to a sticky end."

The Whistle Inn, near Garn-yr-erw

Waun Afon bog to the north-west of the *Whistle Inn*

It was near the *Whistle Inn* that Hywel's relation and enemy, Kent Mortimer stepped into a bog and lost his life: *"Covered with the mud of the bog, I crouched there, watching as he slowly slipped out of my sight, his arms waving; his mud-filled mouth babbling incoherently. I knew no pity, only relief; my children were safe at last: the bog sucked."*

Construction of the Garnddyrys Forge and Rolling Mill

"Up at Garndyrus on the road to Abergavenny, things were happening quickly. This was a new venture by the Blaenafon Iron Company. Balance ponds were sunk, puddling furnaces would be in blast there; the modern rolling mill would replace the drop-hammer system for making finished iron; Garndyrus iron would be the purest in the Eastern Valley, comparable only with that of Merthyr's genius."

The directors of the Blaenafon Ironworks Company have put Hywel in charge of the building of a new rolling mill at Garnddyrus. Blaenafon furnaces would now produce pig iron and this would be sent by tram-road to the new Garnddyrus mill for rolling.

"Swarming with builders now, and under my management, the mill shot up: a row of workers' cottages were built opposite the Works, and a new cottage for me opposite the Garndyrus Inn, later called the Queen's when Victoria came to the throne."

"I supervised the boring of the Pwll-du tunnel that connected Garndyrus to Blaenafon, and through it came the housewives on their way to Abergavenny market: I planned Garndyrus Square of twenty houses; the Row of fifteen more and the Ten Houses for the incoming Blaenafon specialists: I helped to build (but not design) the Blorenge Incline, down which poured 300 tons of finished iron a week for the journey by barge to Newport.

  Garndyrus flowered and was profitable: its puddling fires lit the Usk Valley from Goetre Poorhouse to Crickhowell."

"With the Abergavenny to Brecon Canal now extended to serve Newport, it was being used by inland farmers to transport wheat and barley to the docks by barge; the tonnage being under compulsory requisition by the central government at a fixed price. More, it was officially ordered that such barge loads be weighbridge-checked at Llanfoist, the Garndyrus Company's wharf."

Reconstruction by Michael Blackmore of Garnddyrys in about 1850

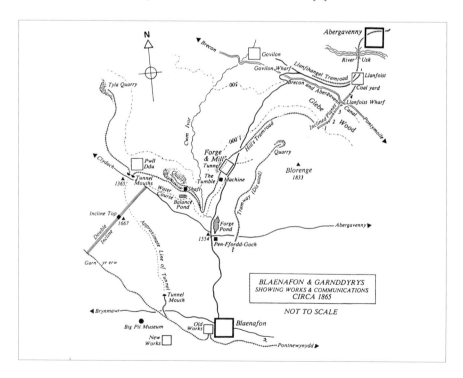

BLAENAFON & GARNDDYRYS
SHOWING WORKS & COMMUNICATIONS
CIRCA 1865

NOT TO SCALE

The novel concludes with Hywel's son Iestyn starting work at Garnddyrus and we enter the pages of *Rape of the Fair Country*, but with the story now being told by Hywel.

"I thought, as I took him round the Tumble tram-road: there lies in this one, in all children, the innocence that the world has lost. And it was this very innocence that the world exploited.

On that dawn walk we found ourselves, as usual, surrounded by scores of children: half-asleep, ragged, and unkempt, they rose up as if from holes in the ground about us.

These were the ore-scrabblers, vagrant Irish mainly, aged from six to fifteen or so, who worked in all weathers on surface veins, digging the iron off the face of the mountain. In their tatters they came, their empty bellies branded on their wan faces, their drumstick limbs projecting obscenely out of their clothes."

"Lurching along beside us on the tram-road, in front and behind us, they slowly emerged into a small tatterdemalion army; the trammers and hauliers of the Pwll-du levels: six-year olds huddled against their sisters to escape the mountain wind."

"As I walked among the thronging child-labour, seeing them with a new eye now my own son was one of them, there grew in my imagination a mirage of beauty that supplanted the sum of misery."

"And it seemed to me.... as if a new dawn was breaking over the earth: one that held in its arms comfort, not only for my crucified generation, but for Iestyn's. Aye, I thought, the family first and last; for me this will always be. Yet I knew in my racing heart that this would not always be: that I was responsible for a million other sons; those who sprang from the loins of men and women who came after me, long after me, my sons and their sons had gone to dust.

One day I thought... things would be changed. Wales would be purged of the cancers that had spread across her body."

John Frost

REQUIEM FOR A PATRIOT

The coming hope, the future day, when Wrong to Right shall bow,
And hearts that have the courage, man, to make the future now.

Ernest Jones

About six weeks after the publication of *This Proud and Savage Land* Alex rang me up and said that he was now ready to start work on another book but did not have anything definite in mind. Could I suggest something that he could really get his teeth into?

I told him that I would give the matter some thought and ring him in a few days if I had any bright ideas. It was not long before the thought struck me that we were approaching a very important anniversary. In three years time it would be the 150th anniversary of the Chartists' uprising. Alex had reminded us of this important historical event in *Rape of the Fair Country*, as seen through the eyes of Iestyn Mortymer.

It would be very interesting to give the subject a different slant by writing a book about the life of John Frost, who was the inspiration behind the march on Newport in 1839 and I knew that Alex had a high regard for him.

When I rang him up, just two days after his call I said, "Alex, I think I've got an idea that should prove of great interest to you."

"Okay, let's hear it," he said.

I replied, "In just three years time, Newport will be celebrating the 150th anniversary of the Chartists' march on the town and the attack on the Westgate Hotel. I think it would be very appropriate if you were to help commemorate this historic event by writing a novel, telling the story of the life of John Frost."

"That's a wonderful idea - you have really hit the nail on the head - I will sit down tomorrow and write a synopsis and send it off to my publisher. It is the ideal subject for me to tackle next for John Frost is one of my heroes and to tie in with such an important anniversary will be simply marvellous.

It will be the story of a man of high ideals who led a movement, threatening revolution in Wales. I will tell the story of his trial in Monmouth Assizes and how he was at first sentenced to death, but then given a reprieve and transported to Van Dieman's land to suffer appalling exile on the other side of the world. I can't wait to get started - it really is the ideal project for me."

Dear Chris

"At the present I am as arid as a desert; no flowers bloom on this particular tree: I am short on energy and bereft of creative thought; the very prospect of entering the soul of John Frost is an anathema, and every time I awake in the morning I see the old bugger looking at me, and his eyes say, 'Don't you dare.'

My working title is *But We shall Rise Again*, but I have no doubt that it will end up as something else.

I hope all is well with you."

In November 1988, the publication of *Requiem for a Patriot* chronicling the life of John Frost leader of the South Wales Chartists' movement was celebrated at the Westgate Hotel, Newport. The chosen day was the 149th anniversary of the Chartists' uprising which took place in Westgate Square with the hotel itself being a focal point of the event.

The book opens in January 1840 with John Frost, William Jones and Zephaniah Williams in the condemned cell of Monmouth Prison.

Cordell describes how John Frost lies on his bed in the cell awaiting the coming dawn. The only sound to be heard was distant hammering and the steady breathing of his fellow prisoners. The prospect of death did not terrify him but it frightened him into cold sweats of anticipation. So much had happened; catastrophe had followed calamity with such monotonous precision in the past weeks, that he now felt that little more could happen to them.

They were unaware at this point that the Queen had in fact reprieved them, and had remitted the death sentence to one of life imprisonment by transportation to Van Dieman's Land.

The action of the book comes in flash backs, and it is in the second half that John Frost tells of his early years as the son of a publican, who owned the *Royal Oak* in Thomas Street, Newport. He leads on to his time among the London radicals, the rise of Chartism; the march on Newport; his transportation to Van Dieman's Land and the seventeen years that he spent there, to eventually return in triumph to Newport, his place of birth.

Alex issued a press release explaining his purpose in writing this book and it read as follows:

"One name rings out like a clarion call in the history of Newport's existence - that of John Frost, draper, magistrate and mayor in the mid-1830s. Certainly no other personality so dominated the port's roll of rags to riches in terms of commercial and social change.

Loved by the oppressed, despised by the ruling classes and feared by the aristocracy, John Frost's fury at the obnoxious Poor Law Act of 1834 turned him from a peace-loving civic dignitary into a dangerous revolutionary who fought for the Six Point Charter of political decency.

John Frost was a moral force character who did not want violence to achieve the aims of the Chartist movement. He was, in fact a very gentle and compassionate man who was much loved and respected by the working class.

The march on Newport was the last bloody revolt in Britain. The Chartist Rebellion has been much underplayed by historians. I am telling the whole story in truth for the first time so that younger people will know who John Frost was and why he was hated by the aristocracy and spurned by the gentry."

John Frost

"Today, the demands of the Chartists would be considered quite mild. They were asking for: Votes for all men, secret ballots, equal electoral districts, no property qualifications for MPs, pay for MPs and annual Parliaments. Such demands were reasonable and this shows that the Chartists were 100 years before their time. Except for annual Parliaments all these points of the Charter are now accepted. I would go so far as to say we owe our democracy to John Frost and the Chartists, the Welsh Chartists in particular."

"I admire John Frost tremendously for he was morally without fault. He could never be corrupted. What I am trying to portray most passionately in my novel is the greatness of this man's life, his suffering and his incredible dominance over fear. *Requiem for a Patriot* tells of the vicious and cruel times when men were fighting for the democracy that we enjoy today.

The beautiful mosaic mural, in John Frost Square, depicting the Chartists' attack on the Westgate Hotel, is more than a tribute to the sacrifices of the forebears of Newport's town fathers; it is the realisation of some years ago of a truth now finally accepted by a new age of historians., that this was was not the vanguard of a failed revolution, the beginning of the end. It was in Churchillian terms, the end of a beginning that was bought by blood."

> "Oh ye who love glory, we heed not the story
> of Waterloo won with the blood of the brave
> But we dare the rough storm, in the cause of reform
> Then let the red banner triumphantly wave."

Welsh Chartist song 1839

The Chartists' Trial at Monmouth

The arrival of John Frost in Monmouth on Saturday 9th November 1839, was reported in the *Monmouthshire Merlin:-*

"This morning (Wednesday) a little before eleven o' clock, Mr. Frost and Mr. Charles Waters were brought to this town, accompanied by a party of 12th Lancers. They were in two carriages and were brought off at once to the County Gaol, where they now lie secured. It was apprehended that an attempt might be made to rescue them but no such thing occurred. The road from Newport to Monmouth was quite tranquil, not a Chartist to be seen.

There is at present a large guard of constables at the gaol. It will be kept up during the night, and until the military arrive. Should anything further occur I shall communicate it to you. It is the opinion now in some quarters that an attempt might be made upon the gaol, so there will be no relaxation in the precautions which have hitherto been taken."

The Monnow Bridge in Monmouth stands at the entrance to the town and in November 1839 the small room above the archway was occupied by Redcoats with muskets at the ready just in case an attempt was made by the Chartists to march on Monmouth in an attempt to fre the prisoners.

Monmouth Gaol was described in the *Monmouthshire Merlin* on 11th January 1840 as follows:-

"It is finely and strikingly situated on the southern slope of a hill, amid a portion of the loveliest scenery of this county, and its elevation above the adjacent meadows is beautifully picturesque. The surrounding hills and eminences clothed with verdant wood, and the sheltered situation, will warrant us in asserting that for salubrity it is not excelled by any prison in the kingdom. The bold and frowning building itself reminds one of feudal ages and it may be considered as having the appearance of one of the ancient fortresses of the kingdom, about the fourteenth century. It is of plain appearance, without any distinctive architectural feature, but is a strong rusticated structure, and so admirably calculated for defence that a military gentleman declared ten artillery-men would successfully hold it against ten thousand insurgents. The prison or interior keep is flanked with massive towers, and the inner apartments are well arranged and adapted to the safe custody of the unfortunate persons who have infringed the laws of their country."

The trial of John Frost, Zephaniah Williams and William Jones began on 31st December 1839, and lasted twenty four days. Twenty prisoners had been charged with treason and fourteen were committed for trial.

The following gentlemen of Monmouthshire were sworn on the Grand Jury: Lord Granville, Charles Henry Somerset (Foreman), The Hon. William Powell Rodney, Llanfihangel Court; Sir Benjamin Hall, Bart., of Llanover Court; William Addams-Williams, of Llangibby Castle; Reginald James Blewitt, of Llantarnam Abbey; Joseph Bailey of Glanusk Park; Richard Blakemore, of the Leys, near Monmouth; William Curre, of Itton Court, near Chepstow; Richard Amphlett Esq., Francis Chambre, Esq.; Phillip John Ducarel, Esq.; Samuel Homfray, of Glenusk; John Francis Vaughan, of Courtfield; John Jenkins of Caerleon; Thomas Lewis of St Pierre, Chepstow; Charles Octavius Swinnerton Morgan, The Friars, Newport; Charles Marriott, of Newton, Monmouth; Francis Mc'Donnell, of Plas Newydd, Usk; Joseph Needham, Abersychan; Charles Harrison Powell Esq.; John Etherington, Esq.; Welch Rolls, of the Hendre, Monmouth; Joseph Davies Esq. and John Gisborne Esq. A total of 250 witnesses were called.

Four counts were brought against the prisoners, the substance of the charge being that they had broken their faith and true allegiance to the Sovereign, and levied war against her within her realm.

The Shire Hall Monmouth is where the Chartist prisoners were tried

Court Room Scene at the trial of the Monmouthshire Chartists

The Counsel for the Crown were Sir John Campbell (Attorney-General), Sir Thomas Wilde (Solicitor-General), Mr Sergeant Ludlow, Mr Sergeant Talfourd, Mr Wightman, and the Hon J. C. Talbot. Sir Frederick Pollock and Mr Fitzroy Kelly defended John Frost. All the prisoners pleaded "not guilty."

The death sentence was passed on John Frost, William Jones, Zephaniah Williams, Charles Walters, John Rees, Richard Benfield, Jenkin Morgan, and John Lovett. Others were charged with treason and sedition and were sentenced to various terms of imprisonment, or acquitted.

There is no doubt that the press made it impossible for the prisoners to receive a fair trial, for all reports declared them guilty of high treason before they were even tried. The *Merthyr Guardian* even commented that if the bodies of traitors were quartered, one of John Frost's limbs could be placed over Pontypool Park, another over Llanover, a third over the door of the council chamber at Newport, and a fourth over the Home Office, the government department that had made Frost a magistrate!

On Thursday 16th January, 1840, the defendants were brought to the Bar to receive sentence. The court was crowded as soon as the doors opened and at nine o' clock the judges took their seats and put on their black caps. It fell to Lord Chief Justice Tindal to pronounce their sentence of death in the following words:-

" It has been proved in your case that you combined together to lead from the hills at the dead hour of night, into the town of Newport, many thousands of men, armed, in many instances, with weapons of dangerous description in order that they might take possession of the town, and supersede the lawful authority of the Queen, as a preliminary step to a more general insurrection throughout the kingdom.

It is owing to the interposition of Providence alone that your wicked designs were frustrated. Your followers arrive by daylight, and, after firing upon the civil power, and upon the Queen's troops, are by the firmness of the magistrate, and the cool determined bravery of a small number of soldiers, defeated and dispersed. What would have been the fate of the peaceful inhabitants of that town, if success had attended your rebellious designs, it is impossible to say. The invasion of a foreign foe would, in all probability have been less destructive to property and life. It is for the crime of High Treason, committed under these circumstances, that you are now called upon yourselves to answer; and by the penalty which you are about to suffer, you hold out a warning to all your fellow subjects, that the law of your country is strong enough to repress and punish all

Chief Justice Tindal, who presided at the trial of
the Chartist leaders at Shire Hall, Monmouth

attempts to alter the established order of things by insurrection and
armed force; and that those who are found guilty of such treasonable
attempts must expiate their crime by an ignominious death."

"That you John Frost and you Zephaniah Williams, and you William
Jones, to be taken thence to the place from which you came and
thence be drawn on a hurdle to the place of execution, and that each
of you be hanged there by the neck until you are dead, and
afterwards the head of each of you will be severed from his body,
and the body of each divided into four quarters, shall be disposed of
as Her Majesty shall think fit, and may Almighty God have mercy
on your souls."

The *Hereford Times* commented:

"Frost still maintained his superiority although his face was ghastly
pale. He sat down without a tremor. Williams hung down his head,
his dark visage expressing the greatest anguish, he fell back upon the
seat, dropping his head upon his hand and, resting his arms upon
his knees, groaned audibly, while William Jones vainly striving to
mask his feelings, trembled in every limb, a deathly paleness spread
over his cheeks, his lips changed to a livid hue... his whole person
showed the fallen man."

The executions of the three men were ordered by the Government to take place at Monmouth on the 6th of February and the executioner and a headsman travelled to Monmouth to prepare the scaffold.

Meanwhile the Chartist Leaders spent three weeks in the condemned cell, sharing one room at their own request. Their ages at this time were: John Frost 54, Zephaniah Williams 48 and William Jones 30.

Numerous petitions from different parts of Britain were presented to the Government on the prisoners' behalf and in acknowledgement to this national campaign to save the lives of the three leaders, a reprieve was granted just four days before their execution was due to take place.

However, it was a reprieve and not a pardon. The Queen remitted the capital sentence upon the condition that the prisoners were transported for the rest of their natural lives.

The young Queen was about to be married and it was no doubt felt that the Royal clemency might well be exercised at such a time for it would be a popular move. Hanging the three ringleaders would no doubt have sparked more revolts, so the establishment decided to transport them to Tasmania in the hope that they might soon be forgotten.

Transportation to Australia was started in 1788 and extended to Tasmania in 1803. It was a punishment for a wide range of offences, often very trivial. The sentences were for 7 years, 14 years or life, and very few returned home. A total of 160,000 people were transported to Australia, including 25,000 women before it was stopped. There were no further transportations to Tasmania after 1853.

Transportation to Tasmania

During a stormy night on 2nd February 1840, the prisoners were roused from sleep, taken to the gaoler's room, and then bundled into a horse-drawn van, handcuffed, chained and guarded by six London policemen and an escort of twenty-four soldiers of the 12th Lancers.

Without being allowed to bid farewell to their families they were conveyed to Chepstow and put on the steamer *Usk* in the custody of their gaoler and guarded by 19 soldiers of the 19th Regiment, who had been waiting to accompany the prisoners to Portsmouth. The prisoners were brought here in great secrecy to avoid attempts of freeing them by other Chartists.

The *Usk*, a paddle steamer of 129 tons, built in 1838, left Chepstow at 6.00 am the following morning, but ran into a gale and then had to put into Ilfracombe for repairs which took two days. Eventually the steamer arrived in Portsmouth where the prisoners were transferred to a prison hulk called 'York' and dressed in convict clothes.

On 24th February, Frost, Williams and Jones, with 210 other convicts were taken aboard the *Mandarin* convict ship at Spithead. Two days later the ship put into Falmouth having lost a topmast. When repairs had been carried out the vessel then set sail on a four month voyage to Port Arthur, Tasmania, otherwise known as Van Dieman's Land.

They arrived in Hobart Town on 30th June 1840. As political prisoners they had certain privileges, being kept off hard physical labour and allowed to keep their own clothes. Frost was sent to Port Arthur, where he became a clerk in the office of Commandant Booth. He was then 56 years old. Zephaniah Williams became a superintendent in the coal mines and William Jones an overseeer blacksmith in the boys' penitentiary at Port Puer.

Harbour and prison buildings, Port Arthur, picture supplied by G. Feeney

On 21st July 1840 Frost wrote a letter to his wife Mary, in England, in which he commented that he was not sent to Port Arthur for punishment, 'but to fill certain offices'. He wrote: "The labour has not been heavy. I am in excellent health - I never was better; and my spirits are very good, considering all things - much better than I could possibly have anticipated. The climate is, so far as I have seen, very good; milder, I expect than our own country;... and from what I hear, I think Port Arthur is a very healthy place."

Frost was transferred to Brown's River (Kingston) late in 1841 and on 22nd November he committed the only offence recorded against his name in Van Dieman's Land: using improper and insolent language to the superintendant of convicts, for which he received three days' solitary confinement. It was recommended that he be sent to Port Arthur but he went instead to Impression Bay (now Premaydena) to work 'in the same manner as other convicts'. He was appointed schoolmaster and eventually made the acquaintance of James Purslowe, Superintendent.

Purslowe commented that, Frost was "studious, quiet and obedient ... attentive to his duties". He was released on probation on 17th November 1843 and worked for a number of private employers in Hobart Town and Bothwell until given his ticket-of-leave in 1846. He was a teacher for eight years at various places until in 1854 he received a conditional pardon. Six months later, he sailed for America with his daughter Catherine, who had recently joined him in exile. At New York in May 1856, at the close of the Crimean War, he received news of his free pardon.

After sixteen years of exile, pardons were indeed granted to all three men but William Jones and Zephaniah Williams decided to stay in Tasmania. Jones went back to work at his old trade of watchmaking but died of poverty in 1873.

Zephaniah Williams joined the police at Newfolk in 1844 and he was recommended to the island Governor by colleagues and onlookers when he calmed seventy lunatics who tried to burn down their hospital and run amok in the town.

He later became a successful coal owner and his trading figures for the last year of his life alone showed a business turnover of £25,000. In his last year of trading he had grossed a massive £18,000! His payroll numbered more than 600 men.

Zephaniah Williams died at Launceston in Tasmania on 8th May 1874 at the age of 82. His son Llewellyn remained in Blaina and was for many years the landlord of the *Rolling Mill Inn*.

John Frost Returns to Newport

On 11th August 1856 John Frost stepped off the Bristol Packet at Rodney Wharf, Newport, to the cheers of a large welcoming crowd. Seated in a carriage decked with flowers. The horses were removed and the carriage was drawn by men in triumph through the town. Outside the *Westgate Hotel*, the large crowd gave him a mighty cheer and Frost was then taken to *The Temperance Hotel* (now demolished) in Llanarth Street where he made a speech from an upstairs window. He told the attentive gathering that his opinions had not changed in the seventeen years that had passed, for there could be no change in a man whose convictions were based on principle. He was determined to work for a radical reform of Parliament as well as for much needed changes to the convict system.

An even greater ovation awaited Frost in London. He was met by a carriage and four at London Bridge and taken to Finsbury Square. The demonstration was so large that *The Times* devoted two full columns to it and estimated that there were 20,000 people present.

By now Frost was 72 years of age and he spent his remaining years writing and lecturing on his experiences as a convict. The text of these lectures were printed as *Horrors of Convict Life* (London 1856) and *A Letter to the People of Great Britain and Ireland on Transportation* (London 1857). During the latter years of his long life he saw the abolition of the property qualifications for election to Parliament, for the Reform Bill of 1867 had given the vote to a large proportion of working men. Frost gradually gave up public life and lived quietly with his family at Stapleton, near Bristol. In his eighty-ninth year he had a bad fall from which he never really recovered and he died on 27th July 1877, at the age of 93 years.

Gradually five points of the Charter were achieved, but it was not until 1918 that the fifth point was won. This gave the vote to all men over the age of 21 years and a decade later through the efforts of the suffragette movement all women over the age of 21 were given the vote as well. The request for Annual Parliaments was really a non-starter for no one would want the upheaval of elections every year.

Newport celebrated the centenary of the Chartists' uprising in 1939 and also the 150th anniversary in 1989. Children recreated the march down Stow Hill to the *Westgate Hotel*, where the commemorative sculpture was unveiled. The anniversary was celebrated throughout Gwent and Glamorgan with a series of events designed to inform, educate and entertain.

An exhibition in Ebbw Vale Civic Centre, entitled Chartism in Blaenau Gwent set out to illustrate how important the Chartist movement was to the people of the industrial towns of Ebbw Vale, Brynmawr, Tredegar and Abertillery.

In October, the Dolman Theatre in Newport hosted a play presented by Newport Playgoers entitled *Never See the Day*. It examined the Chartist movement through the eyes of the leaders and their supporters.

In November the Dolman Theatre put on a play entitled *The Sunday Boys* which was about John Frost and performed by the New Venture Players.

Gwent Theatre toured the county with their specially commissioned play about the Chartist movement. A Chartist Study Week was held at the Gwent College of Higher Education, Allt-yr-yn, with talks given by some of the best-known authors and researchers of the Chartist movement.

Monmouth Museum staged an exhibition entitled *High Treason*, illustrating the trial and transportation of the Chartist leaders.

Cyfarthfa Castle in Merthyr Tydfil put on an exhibition looking at all aspects of the movement in the town and the surrounding area.

* * * * * * * * * * *

NEW DEVELOPMENTS

The Cordell Country Inn

In 1985 a new pub and restaurant was opened near the site of the former Garnddyrys village and forge, overlooking the valley which stretches down from Pwlldu to Govilon and Llanfoist.

The owners, Margaret and Graham Jones had lived in a house on the site for about three years and had an extension built to provide the new pub and restaurant. It was their first venture into the licensed trade.

I remember calling at their house with Alexander Cordell a few months before it opened and they were of course delighted to meet the famous author whose book *Rape of the Fair Country* had made the locality so well known.

The pub which had been kept by Graham's father many years previously had been called the *Royal Oak*, but it had been closed for some considerable time. Whilst we were drinking tea in their lounge, I suggested that it might be a good idea to give the pub a new name that would provide a link with *Rape of the Fair Country*. Alex voiced his agreement, stressing that it would certainly help to boost trade.

Graham said that he would give the matter some thought. He rang me up the next week and told me that they had decided to call it the *Cordell Country Inn* and asked if I could arrange for Michael Blackmore to paint some signs just like the cover on my book. Unfortunately they were not there for long. One was stolen before it was properly erected and the other was vandalised.

The *Cordell Country Inn* was to be officially opened by Alexander Cordell on the 15th of December. He had agreed to fly over from the Isle of Man specially for the occasion. However, a few days before this date he rang me up and I had great difficulty in recognising his voice for he was suffering from influenza. It was obvious that he would not be able to come, and he asked me to stand in for him and perform the opening.

It was a Saturday night and the lounge was crammed with people who had arrived from places like Blaenavon, Brynmawr, Govilon and Gilwern, all expecting to see their favourite author. I made a short speech, explaining that Cordell had been taken ill and then read a brief statement from him praising the enterprise of the new landlords and wishing the new pub every success. He promised that whenever he was in the area he would make a point of visiting the *Cordell Country Inn* and making use of the excellent accommodation that was now available. Also, he maintained that even after his death he would be returning to his favourite part of Wales to become the pub's permanent resident ghost!

Alex certainly kept his word for in the years to come, he and Donnie made frequent visits to this pub and always enjoyed sitting in the lounge, pint of beer in hand, talking to the regulars and visitors, who were always delighted to see him and listen to his fascinating stories.

I was to meet him there on countless occasions and we always had much to talk about. On one occasion we had a conversation about writing techniques and the importance of getting ones facts right. With Alex's agreement, I recorded our conversation and the following is an extract:

"As you well know, my books are all based on careful research in public libraries and I make use of public health records, company records - in fact anything that relates to the period. I try not to give the reader too much history, yet at the same time provide enough history to satisfy those who have a particular knowledge of the event.

It has always been my aim to tell present generations of industrial towns such as Blaenafon, and Merthyr Tydfil, of the social conditions in which their ancestors lived.

For example, in Aberdare, an inspector found five beds in one room at a hovel where the ceiling was so low that the males and females all bundled together could not even sit up.

In 1959, when *Rape of the Fair Country* was first published I had some very severe critics - men who think I have been very salacious. I took quite a hammering from some quarters and began to wonder whether my sources were wrong. But as my research has proceeded I realised that, if anything, I had understated the case.

As far as possible, I like to visit the places that I am writing about and I remember when I visited Pittsburgh to carry out research for my novel *Race of the Tiger*, I was astounded to find on the east coast of America, place-names like Nantyglo, Brynmawr, Tredegar and Hirwaun, which had been introduced by immigrants who left about the time of the Chartist uprising.

With regard to *This Proud and Savage Land* I feel that it has rounded things off. I have always felt that my Welsh novels have lacked a finishing quadrant that would make them complete as a central work. Your excellent suggestion to write the story of Hywel Mortymer helped me to achieve this.

When writing this novel, I made particular use of the infamous *Blue Books* of 1847 which were compiled by English

The Cordell Country Inn opened in 1986

Alexander Cordell sitting inside the bar with his picture on the wall behind him commissioners sent into Wales to report on the state of education.

On the few occasions when the commissioners temporarily forgot their dislike of the Welsh, there creeps in a little of the horror and total exploitation to which Welsh workers were subjected. It is this aspect on which I was able to draw.

It is my opinion that in order to write successfully you have to write about what you know and feel. The three ingredients for writing a novel are sincerity, simplicity and humility."

Alexander Cordell was certainly a diligent researcher and this is proved by his novel *The Fire People*, published in 1972. During his programme of research for this novel he persisted in finding vital evidence to prove that Dic Penderyn, the martyred hero of the 1831 Merthyr Rising was innocent of the crime for which he was hanged. The vital evidence, buried in Home Office Files, had not been previously revealed.

It was Alex's opinion that: "the English government, terrified of being involved in a full scale British revolution, had to find someone to hang as an example to all would-be radicals - and Melbourne, the prime minister, chose Dic Penderyn."

The historian Gwyn Alf Williams in his preface to his book *The Merthyr Rising*, paid Cordell a fine tribute: "As far as South Wales in our times is concerned, it is evidently Alexander Cordell who is the People's Remembrancer."

Alexander Cordell

The First Stage Play of *Rape of the Fair Country*

In October 1987 the Cardiff based Chrysalis Theatre Company premiered the first stage production of *Rape of the Fair Country* at the Newport Lesure Centre. This was also the first time that this centre had been used to stage a play.

The script was written by 27 year old Philip Michell, a graduate of the Welsh College of Music and Drama, and Cordell gave the work his full approval.

"His script is one of which I thoroughly approve. They gave me a long time to consider it, but I read it through from the beginning to end. I was quite happy for this young man to adapt it - he's very sensitive and a very good writer. I think that people are going to like it very much indeed."

A few days later, before the opening night, I was asked to meet the cast for lunch at the *Cordell Country Inn* and take them for a short walk around Garnddyrys and tell them about the history of the area and how I came to write my book *Cordell Country*.

It seemed uncanny to be walking around that beautiful landscape with the characters from the book such as Iestyn, Hywel and Morfydd; Mostyn Jenkins, Tomos Trahearne, Mari Dirion etc..

We staged the fight scene by Keeper's Pond and I took photographs of the cast on the site of the old Garnddyrys Forge and even perched some of them on top of the 'Monster' slag heap. It was an experience that I will never forget.

I was there at the opening night and saw the play again a few weeks later in Hereford. It was also performed at the Taliesin Arts Centre, Swansea; the Parc and Dare Theatre, Treorchy; Wyeside Arts Centre, Builth Wells; and the Sherman Theatre, Cardiff.

"The play is faithful to the ideals of the book - a tribute not to our generation, but to the people of the past who, by their sacrifice and courage, built the Farewell Rock upon which stands the industrial greatness that is Wales today. Yes, the Welsh of Merthyr and Abercarn, Aberdare and Brynmawr; Hirwaun down to Swansea - these are magic names: a people who fought and died for the Six Point Charter, some of which we still enjoy today.

I salute the young actors who have picked up the torch to ensure that those who made Wales great are not forgotten."

Alexander Cordell October 1987

Cast members of the first stage play of *Rape of the Fair Country* visiting the site of Garnddyrys Forge

Members of the cast perched on the slag heap at Garnddyrys

The Discovery of John Frost's Grave

In 1985 Richard Frame, a founder member of Newport Local History Society, undertook some fascinating detective work which led to the discovery of John Frost's grave in a small churchyard at Horfield, Bristol. He later described how he set about his self imposed task:

> "Everything was known about John Frost except where he was buried. We knew he had lived in Stapleton in Bristol, but when we went through various churchyards we couldn't find his grave anywhere. Eventually we tracked down his will to Newport Library and in it he said that he wanted to be buried with his wife Mary and his stepson Henry Hunt."

Richard then returned to Horfield Parish Church in North Bristol, where he found a grave with Henry Hunt's name visible on it. Mary Frosts's name had been obliterated so it was only through the discovery of the will that the grave was identified.

A 45-minute service of dedication, conducted by Canon Wilson of Horfield, was held on 9th October 1986 and afterwards a new tombstone was unveiled by Neil Kinnock, leader of the Labour Party. The slate and granite stone had been donated by Newport Borough Council and carved by Les Thomas and Brian Jarvis of Newport.

After removing a Welsh flag from the new tombstone, Neil Kinnock said:

> "We all owe an immense debt of gratitude to Newport's History Society. John Frost's contribution to history was huge. He was a man of sufficient vision and character to give a real lead and to show that the Chartists were the real voice of the working class rather than just vagabonds. His impact is there today, every time you put a cross on a ballot paper and nobody asks you what your property situation is!"

It was during this ceremony that Neil Kinnock revealed that the new symbol for the Labour Party would be the red rose. It had been chosen because it was the flower placed on the unmarked graves of the Chartists killed by Dragoons in Newport.

The custom of laying red roses on the north side of the graveyard at St Woolos Cathedral in memory of the ten Chartists buried there, began in 1840. This tradition continued for many years but then lapsed. It was revived in 1987 by three members of Newport Local History Society and a year later roses were also laid there on behalf of Neil Kinnock, Paul Flynn MP for Newport West and David Jones, author of *The Last Rising*.

Labour Leader, Neil Kinnock unveiling the new headstone commemorating John Frost at Horfield Parish Curch, near Bristol, in October 1986 - Photograph by Richard Frame

A Chartist Evening in Newport

On the 5th January 1990 Newport Maritime Trust organised a special evening in the Newport Leisure Centre to celebrate the 150th anniversary of the Chartist Uprising of November 1839. The programme of events contained an introduction by Alexander Cordell which read as follows:

"Rape of the Fair Country, initially taken to the hearts of the Welsh people, is now read widely all over the world. From the day of its publication 30 years ago, it has achieved all that a writer could ask of a bestseller: over twenty foreign translations, innumerable book clubs at home and abroad, repeated serialization by print and radio and its film rights sold. To date no film has been made of it because, say the film moguls, its scope in modern terms would demand too expensive a budget.

But they do know, and so do I, that the reason it has not reached the screen is almost purely political. It is now generally regarded that revolutionary ethics (The book tells of the Chartists' attempt to form a republic in Britain) are rarely profitable at the box office: don't rock the boat being the Establishment's cry.

The same applies to television interest: it is widely accepted that the media is to a large extent Government controlled, whatever the protests of its executives: which makes it fortunate that there are still avenues available by which it is possible further to project the popularity of a book which has never been out of print (save for reprint delays) since publication.

1989, being 150 years since the attack on the Westgate, we began to wonder how best the book could be further exploited. Remembering the success of the Dickens reading by the late Emlyn Williams, it was decided to ask Paul Flynn, MP to undertake the task and to this he agreed.

It is hoped that the readings will give you pleasure, but the evening will be something more than this: Chris Barber, the Gwent author, will also be showing his excellent Cordell Country presentation and Rozi and Rob Morris will be performing Chartist songs (composed by this husband and wife team). This will do much to create an evening of drama and music; always the essence of good Anglo-Welsh entertainment.

Being thankful that we did not live in those days when our forebears fought for the things we take for granted today, sit back and enjoy it."

Iestyn Mortymer Returns to Wales

"For 34 years I was constantly asked what happened to Iestyn Mortymer, who was being taken to Monmouth Jail at the end of 'Rape of the Fair Country'. At last I am now able to provide an answer in a new book entitled 'Beloved Exile'."

Alexander Cordell 1993

We were all under the impression that Iestyn had been killed whilst trying to escape when being taken in a cart to Monmouth Jail after the fateful Chartist attack on the Westgate Hotel in Newport in 1839. However, it turns out that he was tried at the Monmouth Assizes and sentenced to twenty-one years transportation for crimes against the Crown.

He is exiled to Afghanistan with Rhys Jenkins and Owen Howells and the story of his adventures is told in *Beloved Exile*, a book (published in 1993) set during the Afghan Wars, which took place between 1839 and 1842 and resulted in 17,000 British soldiers being killed whilst retreating from Kabul.

The story is narrated by Iestyn and Cordell has him consulting his "rain-stained diaries and the ragged manuscript of *Rape of the Fair Country*, which I wrote in Afghanistan."

On arriving in Kabul the three Welshmen are set to work as furnacemen. During his spare time Iestyn is writing the story of his life as related in *Rape of the Fair Country* and at the same time keeping a diary of everything that he experiences in Afghanistan.

All the time he thinks of Wales and memories of his wife Mari keep cropping up in dreams, but he succumbs to temptation and has an affair with the Afghan Princess Durrani.

Iestyn continues to write his autobiography, with memories of life in Blaenafon and the people he once knew flooding back. Snatches from the text of *Rape of the Fair Country* are included from time to time as Iestyn dreams of his homeland.

Eventually, disguised as an Arab gentleman, by the name of Ahmad Saud, he manages to escape on a paddle steamer going down the Indus river and then boards a steamship at Karachi bound for Liverpool.

He then travels by packet steamer to Carmarthen and continues by stage coach to Morfa Bach to find Cae White farmhouse where his family once lived. Arriving there, he learns that his brother Jethro has sailed away to America and that Mari has gone to a place called Resolven in the Neath Valley. He is also told that a man called Shanco Matthews had told Jethro that his brother was dead and that Mari believed that as well.

It was a fifty mile coach journey to Neath, and arriving there Iestyn hires a buggy which takes him to the *Cuddlecombe Inn*, a hostelry on the tow-path of the Tennant Canal. Asking after Mari, he is directed to the *Old Navigation*, near Resolven. But he finds the building derelict and there are no clues to be found of where his wife might have gone. Iestyn returns to his trap and a man standing there is able to inform him that Mari has married Mostyn Evan, a bargee, and that they had left the valley and gone to live at Green Fach, Aberdare.

On arriving in Aberdare, Iestyn is directed to Number Five Green Fach. However, the house is empty and a neighbour ignores his question when he asks after Mari Evan.

He then makes his way to St John's churchyard, where he finds a grave with fresh flowers and a simple wooden tablet with the following inscription:

> MOSTYN EVAN
> SON OF BEN THE
> DROVER
> also
> MARI, HIS WIFE
> Died down Gadlys Pit
> 9th September, 1854
> Interred by their
> comrades
> in the Colliers' Benefit

One can imagine the grief that Iestyn must have felt on reading this inscription. The next day he travels on to Nantyglo, visiting the turmoil of Baileys' iron empire, and standing in the yard of Long Row he looks at the window of what was once their bedroom and remembers the first night of his wedding.

He travels on to Blaenafon and sees the little house in Shepherds Square where his family once lived. It is now getting late and he travels on to spend the night at the *Royal Oak* , which is kept by Selwyn ap Pringle, who first appeared in *This Proud and Savage Land* and by now must be quite elderly.

Next morning, Iestyn sets off again, descending to Fiddlers Elbow and on through Llanfoist to reach Llanelen. Sitting on the river bank, listening to the song of the Usk, he comes to terms with the fact that in this spot, where he first met Mari Dirion, his search had come to an end and that he must come to terms with his sad loss. This is not the end of the book, but a suitable point to finish.

The Excavation of Ty Mawr

In May 1993 Alexander Cordell returned to Nantyglo to unveil a plaque commemorating the excavation of the site of Ty Mawr (one-time home of Crawshay and Joseph Bailey) by pupils of Brynmawr School. The work had been begun in 1981, involving pupils of Nantyglo Comprehensive School, which ironically was built on the site of the old ironworks once owned by the Bailey brothers.

After several years the excavation was taken over by pupils of Brynmawr School and further work was also undertaken by the Gwent Probation Service as a Community Order project.

Alex unveiled the plaque and remarked:

> "My feelings towards the ironmaster Crawshay Bailey are vitriolic. No one is more angry about this man than myself, but we must remember that he was a creature of the time.
>
> At this point in history it was not unusual for young children to work in the mines, or in the ironworks, and while Bailey could be harsh, he was not alone in this.
>
> However, he could be quite different, and on one occasion when a seam of coal was discovered, after a period when he almost faced bankruptcy, Bailey rode all the way to Abergavenny and borrowed money from his bank to pay his workers."

The Regeneration of Blaenafon

In September 2000, I was asked to perform the official opening of Butterflies Restaurant in Queen Street, Blaenafon. Previously known as the *Cross Keys Inn*, it was credited with the idea of bringing "bar snacks" to the town. According to a local tale dating back to 1891, four hungry young men caught a rat and persuaded the landlady of the pub to cook it in butter for them.

John Morgans, proprietor of the nearby *Cambrian* public house, was responsible for establishing this new restaurant. It was decided to name the new venture 'Butterflies' after a large number of Red Admirals that were found there during the refurbishment.

In my speech at the opening ceremony I said:

"The name Butterflies seems a strange choice for a restaurant but it is in fact quite relevant. For what is a butterfly? It is a beautiful thing that has been reborn - transformed into something else - given a new beginning. Well, that it certainly true in this instance, for the old *Crosskeys Inn* has been changed beyond all recognition. It has been extended, beautifully furnished and tastefully decorated. Complete with patio, fountain and a splendid garden outside, it is just like an oasis in the heart of historic Blaenafon.

I can sense a new feeling of optimism growing in Blaenafon and it is pleasing to see that improvements have really started to happen here, with environmental work being carried out on the edge of the town and the old Council Office at last being restored for use as a new library.

Big Pit has been made the National Mining Museum of Wales and the restoration of the Ironworks, said to be the finest example in Europe, continues to make steady progress. Also, I understand that there is a 95% likelihood that in November it will be announced that Blaenafon with its unique industrial landscape will be awarded World Heritage status. We all await the final decision with great anticipation.

If this declaration does indeed come about, then Blaenafon will **really** be on the map and placed on a list of important places that includes the Great Wall of China and the Taj Mahal. Visitors will be pouring in by the thousand and of course looking for somewhere that serves good food.

Butterflies Restaurant, Queen Street, Blaenafon

The old Council Office in the centre of Blaenafon
has been restored to provide a new library for the town

This is hopefully just the first of many new businesses which will then be opened in the town. So to my mind Butterflies Restaurant represents a symbol of the fresh optimism that is at last beginning to blossom in Blaenafon.

I have always considered Blaenafon to be a very special place and of particular historic importance. During the 19th century it was really thriving, with full employment and, as the birthplace of many advances in technology, it played a major role in furthering Britain's Industrial Revolution.

But Blaenavon has also been put on the map through the novels of Alexander Cordell. This famous author had a special affection for the town and its people, for he frequently roamed the streets in the late 1950s, whilst researching for his novel *Rape of the Fair Country*. Translated into seventeen languages, this book sold millions of copies and people in places as far away as America and Japan have read about Blaenavon and imagined Cordell's colourful characters.

My own book *Cordell Country*, published in 1985, also gave this area a special identity; just like 'Thomas Hardy Country' or 'Kilvert Country'. It was written as a tribute to Alexander Cordell and brought many new visitors to the area. During the last two years I have also been re-publishing some of Alexander Cordell's novels which have been out of print for many years. These titles have included *Rape of the Fair Country* and *This Proud and Savage Land* which are both very important books for promoting Blaenafon.

I also have hopes that one day the film of *Rape of the Fair Country* will at last be made. When that happens, the fame of this town will really be spread far and wide and tourists will flock here to visit the location where the action took place.

If Alexander Cordell was still alive today, I am sure that it would have been he who would have been invited to perform this opening ceremony. But as a local author, who knew Cordell very well, I feel that I am standing in for him and I recall that on a few occasions, during his lifetime, this indeed did happen, when I was asked to perform similar ceremonies on his behalf.

Alex always enjoyed a good meal in a well appointed restaurant and I am sure that he would have been a regular customer to Butterflies if he was still around today.

It now gives me great pleasure to declare the Butterflies Restaurant officially open."

249

Blaenafon Achieves World Heritage Site Status

In the mid 1990's when some thought was being given to the Blaenafon Industrial Landscape becoming a world Heritage Site, Alexander Cordell commented that if this could be achieved it would be a fitting epitaph to the people who died making this small town such an industrial giant. He added: "All that the people of the past have to commend them for the sacrifices they made, are the dirt monuments that they left behind. That is why it is so incumbent on people with influence to sacrifice everything to get this done. There is no town which deserves it better than Blaenafon!"

Thanks to the sterling efforts of the Blaenafon Partnership led by the Torfaen County Borough Council, Cordell's dream of World Heritage Site status was realised on November 30th 2000. On this memorable day the World Heritage Committee of UNESCO, at a meeting at Cairns in Australia inscribed the 'Blaenafon Industrial Landscape' on the list of world Heritage Sites. This was a tremendous achievement bearing in mind that over 500 sites in the UK had expressed a keen interest in becoming World Heritage Sites.

What makes Blaenafon so special is the fact that it has, surprisingly been left virtually untouched by modernisation. The basic fabric of both the town and the surrounding landscape remains intact and provides one of the best preserved industrial landscapes in Britain. Not only does the area contain a large concentration of internationally significant archaeological features: but it provides a fascinating reminder of the important role the people of this part of Wales played in the formative years of the Industrial Revolution.

It must be remembered that it was Alexander Cordell's famous novel, *Rape of the Fair Country*, published in 1959, which brought to people's attention the historic importance of Blaenafon. When he sold the film rights to the book in 1960, the resultant publicity had the effect of saving the ironworks and nearby Stack Square from destruction. Thankfully, the Blaenafon Town Council decided that these crumbling ruins should not be bulldozed and levelled, but retained as a possible film set. Sadly, despite interest shown by the actors Stanley Baker and Richard Burton, the film has never been made, but now perhaps as a result of World Heritage designation, there is a greater chance of such a project being undertaken.

In the early 1990s when some thought was being given to Blaenavon and its surrounding industrial landscape as a possible World Heritage Site, Alexander Cordell commented that if this could be achieved it would be a fitting epitaph to the people who died making this small town such an industrial giant:

"All that the people of the past have to commend them for the sacrifices they made, are the dirt monuments they left behind. That is why it is so incumbent on people with influence to sacrifice everything to get this done. There is no better town which deserves it than Blaenafon."

Industrial landscape near Blaenafon

Death of Alexander Cordell

"My generation had our politics shaped by Alex's accounts of the cruelty and the heroism of the lives of past working class people of South Wales. His vivid writing inspired the outrage we continue to feel about the injustices meted out to our ancestors. He is genuinely irreplaceable and we all owe him a debt of gratitude."

Paul Flynn MP for Newport West

Alexander Cordell went missing from his home in Rhosddu, Wrexham, on July 2nd, 1997 soon after completing his last novel, *Send Her Victorious*. His body was found eight days later by John Roberts, a local farmer, near the Horseshoe Pass, Llangollen, which was a brief car journey from his home.

The body was later identified as that of the well known author Alexander Cordell. It was a strange set of circumstances: near his body was a half-consumed bottle of Napoleon brandy. On his body was found a bottle containing seven Temazepan sleeping pills. Propped up on the haversack in front of him were two photographs, one each of his wives which he was missing so much.

Such items suggested suicide, particularly to the media, yet a medical examination found no traces of drugs or alcohol in his body. He had in fact died of a heart attack.

The north-east Wales coroner, John Hughes commented: "It is ironic in the extreme that a man who was such an exemplary storyteller should have a story about his own life even to the very end."

In fact Cordell's death is almost like the twist in a plot of one of his novels - an elderly author who sets out to commit suicide in a remote spot - but before he can do so is struck down by a heart attack.

It is reminiscent of a scene in *This Proud and Savage Land*, where Hywel Mortymer creeps into his wicked uncle's house, pistol in hand, determined to kill him, but suddenly realises that the figure lying in bed has already passed away through natural causes.

When interviewed by Penny Roberts, Chief Reporter for BBC Wales, I commented:

"Alexander Cordell was a man who not only had an inexhaustible fund of interesting tales to relate, complete with all the appropriate accents, but he also had a great sense of humour. At the same time he was a good listener who took particular pleasure in hearing anecdotes from local people, many of which were subsequently incorporated in his novels.

Wales was his adopted country and he had an insatiable interest in its history, but most of all he set out to record for posterity the hardships and humour of its people. His research was thorough and no other writer has managed to capture the atmosphere and spirit of the people of 19th century industrial Wales so well.

Alex was an exceptional writer who had the ability to make the reader feel that his fictional characters actually existed. He lived for nothing but writing and was never content unless he was working on a book. His enthralling set of novels will ensure that he will live on in our minds through the characters that he created over many years of industrious achievement."

In 1995 Alexander Cordell had realised that he did not have long to live and he drove down from Wrexham to Abergavenny to arrange his own funeral. He ordered a bookmark headstone and composed a suitable epitaph, which commemorates himself and his two wives. All that needed to be added was the date of his death. His ashes were to be buried in the grave of his first wife Rosina.

IN MEMORY
OF
ALEXANDER
CORDELL
WHO DIED
9th JULY 1997

AND
BELOVED WIFE
ROSINA
WHO DIED
20th MAY 1972
The first, the loveliest
and the best,
and then along came
DONNIE
her friend;...to both
wives I owe so much.

Memorial to Alexander Cordell in the cemetery at Llanfoist, Abergavenny

Behind this memorial is the grave of Patrick (Max) Donovan who died in 1960 and his wife Elsie (known as Donnie), who became Cordell's second wife. The two couples had lived next door to each other in Abergavenny and a strong friendship had developed. When Cordell's first wife Rosina died, twelve years after the death of Max Donovan, a strong bond between Donnie and Alex led to them getting married in 1973. Donnie died at the age of 80 in 1995.

BOOKS PLAYS AND MUSICAL PRODUCTIONS

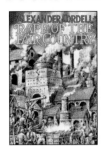  

Republication of the Welsh Trilogy

I knew that Alex was disappointed that his books were no longer available but he was too old to do anything about it and by then was content that they were at least available in public libraries.

People had been ringing me up, to ask where they could get hold of a copy of *Rape of the Fair Country* because they wanted to read it again. I was constantly told by people how years ago they had loaned their copy to someone who had not returned it and they could no longer find the novel in any bookshop.

At the time of his death all Cordell's popular Welsh novels were out of print and the literary rights were in the hands of his daughter Georgina who lived in Finland. I wrote to her saying that I would like to republish some of the books. She wrote back, giving her permission and put me in touch with Alex's solicitor and his London agent.

I felt that a new generation would now be ready to read the books which had become very scarce after his death. The special thing about his Welsh trilogy in particular, is that you can read and re-read these books without getting tired of the stories. I've probably read *Rape of the Fair Country* no less than a dozen times, yet I could still sit down and read it again.

Some of the covers of his novels were pretty awful and anyone picking them up may have been put off, thinking that the books were bodice-rippers rather than serious literature. My artist friend Michael Blackmore of Abergavenny has given the new series a fresh look which is accurate in every respect. Not only are they the best and most appropriate covers that the novels have ever had, but they are beautifully painted and historically accurate. Previously, an artist, not familiar with the period, often depicted a modern steelworks in the background rather than an 18th or 19th century ironworks.

Further Development of Cordell Country

In 1999 seven local authorities in Wales (Neath and Port Talbot, Merthyr, Caerphilly, Rhondda Cynon Taf, Blaenau Gwent, Torfaen and Monmouthshire) joined forces to promote an extended version of 'Cordell Country' to create a series of exciting tourist destinations linked with some of his novels set in the Welsh Valleys. With an EC grant of around £60,000 and with the support of the Wales Tourist Board, the idea became a major literary tourism initiative.

A series of leaflets, audio tapes and interpretative panels were produced to promote the trails linking places where Cordell set his action and characters.

To encourage visitors to stay in the area, a 'Short Breaks in Cordell Country' brochure was also produced.

The First Musical Production of *Rape of the Fair Country*

A musical adaptation by Monmouth-based husband and wife song-writing team Rob and Rozi Morris. The production featured students and staff from Gwent College of Higher Education at Caerleon.

Alexander Cordell was very pleased with the result despite initially believing that it would be beyond the reach of any amateur production. He commented afterwards: "I feared the worst, but at the end people were weeping in the audience and at least two of the women on stage were in tears. I was very moved by the performance and thought it absolutely beautiful."

The Second Musical Production

Writer/composer, Terry Underwood and Alexander Cordell had been friends for many years, first meeting when Terry was doing a production of "Lorna Doone" in Chepstow, and they hit it off straight away. In 1970 Terry set up the Newport Pantomime Society and asked Alex if he would be a vice-president.

On Saturday 27th October, 1997, Terry's theatre company, The New Venture Players held their premiere of a musical version of *Rape of the Fair Country* at the Dolman Theatre in Newport. Alex had been looking forward to being their guest of honour, but sadly died in July of that year. The New Venture Players presented their show as a dedication and memorial to him.

The Clwyd Theatr Cymru Productions

In February 2000 the full Alexander Cordell trilogy: *Rape of the Fair Country,* *Hosts of Rebecca,* and *Song of the Earth* was staged one after the other at Clwyd Theatr Cymru in Mold, providing audiences with about ten hours of theatre in one day.

This millenium project was the biggest event ever seen on a Welsh stage and Alexander Cordell gave the idea his full blessing before he died in 1997.

The three plays were adapted by Manon Eames who had the daunting task of condensing 100,000 words minimum (in each novel) to about 25,00 words of stage playing time. She commented:

'What you leave out becomes as important as what you leave in. But the real challenge lies in being true to two of ten conflicting essentials - on the one hand, the original author's vision and energy - and on the other, the ebb and flow in dramatic structure and narration which is demanded by live theatre.'

The Director Tim Baker commented:

"The experience of creating and staging the three plays has been a fascinating one - a three year immersion in Cordell's own explanation of the forces at work when men and women attempt to improve their circumstances in the face of seemingly impossible odds. Although not a Welshman, Cordell found a spirit and a voice in his novels which transfer to the stage with remarkable intensity."

The three plays were also performed at the New Theatre Cardiff from 7th-24th March of that year, individually and again altogether on Saturday 25th March.

> "*Powerful ensemble acting... another massive contribution to the English language theatre by Welsh-born actors.*"
> Western Mail

> "*One of the most moving theatrical events we are likely to see for some time.*"
> The Daily Post

The Alexander Cordell Literature Competition

On November 7th 2003, a Literature Competition was launched to perpetuate the name of Alexander Cordell. It was open to all writers, published and unpublished and involved a 1,500 upper word limit with South Wales as the subject. The top prize was £500 with the second and third prizes of £300 and £150 respectively.

The competition was supported by all Gwent Councils and those of Merthyr Tydfil, Neath Port Talbot and Rhondda Cynon Taf as well as Capital Regional Tourism, Academi, Blaenafon Booktown and the European Regional Development Fund.

The Blaenafon Community Heritage and Cordell Museum

This visitor centre has been established in part of the Library building to ensure that the story of the people of Blaenafon has a place in the town's history. Here also can be seen some of Alexander Cordell's personal writing effects, including his desk and typewriter.

Lion Street, Blaenafon - Telephone: 01495 790991
www.blaenafonheritagemuseum.org.uk

The Blaenafon World Heritage Centre

The Blaenafon World Heritage Centre is situated in the former St Peter's Church School, originally built in 1815 to provide free education for the ironworkers' children. The new centre will continue the educational mission of its predecessor but in a modern and exciting way. It has been financed by the Heritage Lottery Fund and Welsh Assembly Government and will feature displays, film and multi-media screens to help visitors appreciate the significance of Blaenafon's Industrial Landscape.

Within the new heritage centre, a new glass and steel building has been erected to house visitor reception, retail and café areas and to provide a physical link between the two historic buildings - one of which will feature temporary exhibitions, events and educational activities. It will also include facilities for meetings and small conferences.

Built at a cost of £2.7 million, this centre is the first of its kind in the UK and it will provide a focal point for the interpretation of thie Blaenafon Industrial Landscape World Heritage Site which covers an area of 33 square kilometres and was once a couldron of furious activity during the early days of the Industrial Revolution.

Telephone: 01495 742336

FURTHER READING

Barber C.	*Cordell Country* Blorenge Books 1985
Barber C.	*Walks in Cordell Country* Blorenge Books 1993
Barber C. /Blackmore M.	*Portraits of the Past* Blorenge Books 1996
Barber C.	*Eastern Valley - The Story of Torfaen* Blorenge Books 2000
Barber C.	*Exploring Blaenavon Industrial Landscape*
	World Heritage Site Blorenge Books 2002
Bowen R.	*Blaenavon in Old Picture Postcards* European Library1982
Buckingham M./Frame R.	*Alexander Cordell* University of Wales Press, Cardiff 1999
Davies E.J.	*The Blaenavon Story*
	Torfaen Council 1975
Gladwin D.D & J.H.	*The Canals of the Welsh Valleys* The Oakwood Press
Hadfield C.	*The Canals of South Wales and the Border* David & Charles
Jones D.J.V.	*The Last Rising* Clarendon Press Oxford
Lewis J./Thomas M.	*Blaenavon through the years* (Vols 1.2 & 3)
	Old Bakehouse Publications 1987, 1993, 1998
Molloy P.	*And they Blessed Rebecca* Gomer Press 1983
Phillips, D.R.	*The History of the Vale of Neath* Swansea, 1925
Rattenbury G.	*Tramroads of the Brecknock & Abergavenny Canal* 1980
van Laun J.	*The Clydach Gorge* Brecon Beacons National Park 1976
van Laun J.	*Early Limestone Railways* London 2001
Wakelin, P	*Blaenavon Ironworks* Cadw 2006
Williams D.	*John Frost, a Study in Chartism* University of Wales Press,
Williams D.	*The Rebecca Riots* University of Wales Press 1955

ALEXANDER CORDELL

Alexander Cordell (George Alexander Graber) was born on 9th September, 1914 in Sri Lanka, then Ceylon. He was one of four children of Frank and Amelia Blanche Graber. His father was a Regimental Sergeant Major in the Royal Engineers. Educated by the Marist Brothers at Tiensin in China, Alex followed his father into the army in 1932, when he also joined the Royal Engineers. He served in the ranks until 1936 and was then commissioned, attaining the rank of Major during the Second World War.

Seriously injured during the British Expeditionary Force's retreat from Bologne in 1940, he spent his convalescence at Harlech in North in Wales and developed a love and fascination for the country and its people. As a result, after being demobilised in 1950, he went to live in Llanelen, near Abergavenny in Monmouthshire. He was employed as a quantity surveyor with the Ministry of Public Buildings and Works.

In his spare time he began to write short stories and his first novel, *A thought of Honour* was published in 1954. He described it as an attempt to expunge "the dirt of war". Unfortunately, it was not very successful, but his second novel, *Rape of the Fair Country* became an international best-seller, being published in no less than seventeen languages. Cordell in later years commented: "I wrote the book at white heat, scarcely altering a chapter; in between spells of writing I studied at the University of Wales, Aberystwyth, and befriended every available librarian; more, I suddenly discovered that hand in hand with the tale of the mountain town of Blaenavon, went the last bloody revolution, in Britain, the Chartist Rebellion."

Alex was always proud to mention that he had a Welsh speaking grandmother who was born in the Rhondda Valley. His paternal grandfather, was a German, was born in Dusseldorf. On becoming a successful writer, Alex adopted the pseudonym Cordell because Graber sounded too Germanic.

Rape of the Fair Country was the first of a successful trilogy set in 19th century industrial Wales, being quickly followed by *Hosts of Rebecca* and *Song of the Earth*. A second Welsh trilogy was later to follow.

Now established as a successful novelist, Cordell took early retirement and became a full time writer. In total he wrote thirty books, which were set in a variety of locations, but his most popular novels describe the turbulent times of 19th century industrial Wales, for that undoubtedly was his favourite subject.

Rape of the Fair Country has been performed as a play on the stage, and radio and musical versions of the story have also been produced. For over thirty years there has been talk of a film of the book being made and it was always a disappointment to Alexander Cordell that this did not happen during his lifetime. To most people who have read the book it is very surprising that the film has not been made for it would undoubtedly prove very popular.

Alexander Cordell died of a heart attack near Llangollen, North Wales in July 1997. His final novel *Send Her Victorious* was published during the following month.

TITLES BY ALEXANDER CORDELL

A Thought of Honour	1954
Rape of the Fair Country	1959
The Hosts of Rebecca	1960
Race of the Tiger	1963
The Sinews of Love	1965
Song of the Earth	1967
The Bright Cantonese	1967
The Fire People	1972
If You Believe the Soldiers	1973
The Dream and the Destiny	1975
This Sweet and Bitter Earth	1977
To Slay the Dreamer	1980
Rogue's March	1981
Land of My Fathers	1983
Peerless Jim	1984
Tunnel Tigers	1986
Tales from Tiger Bay	1986
This Proud and Savage Land	1987
Requiem for a Patriot	1988
Moll	1990
Beloved Exile	1993
The Dreams of Fair Women	1993
Land of Heart's Desire	1995
The Love that God Forgot	1996
Send her Victorious	1997

For Children
The White Cockade	1970
Witch's Sabbath	1970
The Healing Blade	1971
The Traitor Within	1971
Sea Urchin	1979

TITLES BY CHRIS BARBER

Walks in the Brecon Beacons
Exploring the Waterfall Country
Ghosts of Wales
Exploring the Brecon Beacons National Park
Exploring Gwent
Mysterious Wales
More Mysterious Wales
Cordell Country
The Romance of the Welsh Mountains
Hando's Gwent (Volume 1)
Hando's Gwent (Volume 2)
The Ancient Stones of Wales (Jointly with J.G. Williams)
The Seven Hills of Abergavenny
Journey to Avalon (Jointly with David Pykitt)
Arthurian Caerleon
Abergavenny in Old Picture Postcards
Portraits of the Past
Classic Walks in the Brecon Beacons National Park
In Search of Owain Glyndwr
Eastern Valley - The Story of Torfaen
Exploring Blaenavon Industrial Landscape World Heritage Site
Exploring Kilvert Country
Llanover Country
The Legacy of King Arthur

RELEVANT TITLES AVAILABLE FROM BLORENGE BOOKS

Rape of the Fair Country
by Alexander Cordell (ISBN 1 872730 15 9) – £5.99

Hosts of Rebecca
by Alexander Cordell (ISBN 1 872730 19 1) – £5.99

Song of the Earth
by Alexander Cordell (ISBN 1 8 72730 20 5) – £5.99

This Proud and Savage Land
by Alexander Cordell (ISBN 1 8 72730 21 3) – £6.99

Land of My Fathers
by Alexander Cordell (ISBN 1 872730 36 1 and 9 781872730363) – £5.99

The Fire People
by Alexander Cordell (ISBN 1 872730256) – £6.99

Eastern Valley – The Story of Torfaen
by Chris Barber (ISBN 1 872730 23X) – £15.00

Exploring Blaenavon Industrial Landscape
by Chris Barber (ISBN 1 872730 26 4) – £9.99

To order copies of these books please send cheques (made payable to Blorenge Books) for the above amounts, clearly stating your name and address. Please add £1 per book for postage and packing.

Blorenge Books, Blorenge Cottage, Church Lane,
Llanfoist, Abergavenny NP7 9NG
(Telephone: 01873 856114)

www. blorenge-books.co.uk